The Royal Irish Constabulary:
An Oral History

First published 1990
by the Institute of Irish Studies
The Queen's University of Belfast,
University Road,
Belfast.

This book has received financial assistance under the Cultural Traditions Programme which aims to encourage acceptance and
understanding of cultural diversity.

ISBN 0 85389 340 3

Printed by W. G. Baird, Ltd., Antrim.

The Royal Irish Constabulary: An Oral History

John D. Brewer

The Institute of Irish Studies,
The Queen's University of Belfast

Also by John D. Brewer

Mosley's Men (Gower, 1984).
After Soweto (Clarendon Press, 1987).
Police, Public Order and the State (Macmillan, 1988: co-authored).
Can South Africa Survive? (Macmillan, 1989: editor).
Inside the RUC (Clarendon Press, 1990).

List of Contents

Preface and acknowledgements

I belong to that generation which can remember sitting at the feet of elderly relatives listening to stories about their exploits in the Second World War. This filial memory has left me with a fascination for oral history, which first expressed itself in postgraduate research on former members of the British Union of Fascists. The recollections of the elderly about earlier events are, for me at least, the life blood of history, adding to the insights gained from official documents and archives what Paul Thompson calls the authentic voice of the past.

My work on the Royal Ulster Constabulary first made me aware of the existence of a small band of survivors from the original Royal Irish Constabulary. Their number has dwindled by nearly half since the beginning of the research, to now total just over a dozen. I was eager to record for posterity the testimonies of these lively and engaging characters before their insights were lost forever, and this book is the outcome. It is written in the belief that future generations should have the opportunity to learn something about Ireland's troubled history from the memories of some of the people involved. This has already been done with some of the Volunteers in the Irish Republican Army, and this volume allows policemen to talk of their past involvement in Ireland's conflicts. But the accounts of these policemen also speak to the modern world, for their recollections of policing in rural Ireland at the time of partition resonate in Northern Ireland today. For these reasons it has been my intention to respond to the growing public interest in policing issues in Ireland by writing a book which is free of jargon, has no obsessively detailed footnote citations, and is accessible to a wide readership.

One of the survivors, who, sadly, has since died, first engaged me over the garden fence with tales of life in the Royal Irish Constabulary, but I am indebted to the interest and enthusiasm of many people. Mr Robin Sinclair is owed a special debt of gratitude for helping to locate, and arrange interviews with, over half (at that time) of the surviving members of the force. The Nuffield Foundation are to be thanked for providing funds to undertake the research, on grant number SOC/ 181(1656). Mrs Alice Nesbitt very competently transcribed the interviews. Mr Richard Hawkins read the volume in its entirety with an attention to detail for which I am extremely grateful. But the greatest debt is owed to the fifteen men whose memories are contained herein, and to their families, whose hospitality was warmly received; I am sincere in declaring that this book could not have been written without them.

John D. Brewer
Belfast, 1990

CHAPTER 1

The Royal Irish Constabulary

Introduction

Traditions die hard in Ireland. The vocabularies which give expression to these traditions are equally tenacious; modern terminology is often replete with images of the past. This is nowhere more apparent than in aspects of policing. The history of the Royal Irish Constabulary (RIC) comes to life in Northern Ireland today by the routine use of the term 'barrack' to describe police stations, and by the widespread tendency of policemen in the Royal Ulster Constabulary (RUC) to refer to themselves as 'Robert's men' or 'Peelers'.

Police forces of some description existed in Ireland from earliest times,[1] but most people date the formation of the modern Irish police to 1814, when Mr (later Sir) Robert Peel, Chief Secretary of Ireland, formed the Peace Preservation Force (PPF). However, a county police had existed in scattered baronies since 1773, and Dublin had its own city-wide force from 1778. The separate Irish Constabulary was formed in 1822 as the first national police force. It absorbed the PPF when the various forces were consolidated with the reorganization of the Irish Constabulary in 1836. The following year the police in Dublin were reorganized. In 1867 the Irish Constabulary earned the prefix 'Royal' as a result of its action in containing civil unrest in what is referred to as the Fenian Uprising. The force was disbanded in 1922 with partition, when the RUC replaced it in Northern Ireland and the Garda Siochana in the Irish Republic.

The period of the RIC's existence covered a century that oscillated between peace and protest, turmoil and tranquility, eventually culminating in civil war. The RIC was integrally involved in these events, and the men (there were no policewomen) who comprised the force were some of the significant players in Ireland's drama. A great deal has been written on the RIC's role therein, especially in the political violence leading up to partition,[2] although, surprisingly, no institutional history of the force yet exists, except the volume by Curtis

1

published well over a century ago.[3] The official history of the RIC, therefore, still has to be written. However, there is one other gap in our knowledge. There are some books of personal recollections by officers,[4] the memoirs of constable Jeremiah Mee,[5] and Shea's account of his father's life in the RIC,[6] but the people within the RIC have yet to speak to us directly, whether about life in the force, or the conflicts within which they became embroiled.

This volume seeks to fill the void, and complements the oral history research among nine Volunteers from the Irish Republican Army (IRA) who were active in the civil war.[7] It draws on the recollections of fifteen of the twenty-five policemen from the RIC who were still alive when the research began in 1987; a number now diminished to fifteen. Inevitably, all joined the force in its last years, and their experiences are dominated by the events surrounding partition. Political violence, the militarization of policing, relations with the army, and eventual disbandment are prominent features in their accounts, and are reflected in the contents of this volume. But Ireland's troubles did not completely blot out more ordinary features of police work, about which respondents recall a considerable amount. Sometimes the balance is reversed. Because of the restricted geographical location of much of the political violence, some respondents rarely encountered 'the troubles', and life within the RIC took on the same character as it had decades before. Therefore, mundane features of police work are also addressed here. In an attempt to establish what sorts of people were joining the force at this time, and the motivations for doing so, a chapter focuses on the respondents' upbringing and childhood experiences in rural Ireland at the turn of the century.

The volume is broken into two parts. As a background to the oral history, the rest of this chapter will give a brief outline history of the RIC, while the next discusses the strengths and weaknesses of the oral history method, and introduces the respondents. Part II comprises the oral testimonies, and is organized into a number of chapters which represent the dominant themes in the accounts given by respondents.

A brief outline history of the RIC

Before the formation of Peel's PPF, responsibility for law and order lay with the inefficient and inadequate county police, most of whom were pensioners,[8] whose duties were primarily to service the legal administration of magistrates. Under a 1773 Act, they were required to be Protestant, and the force was never deployed in times of civil unrest, when the military was utilized. The PPF was formed in 1814 because of the drain on military resources caused by the Napoleonic wars, and during the debate in Westminster on the formation of the force Peel objected in principle to the use of soldiers to enforce public peace – a stimulus to his subsequent formation of the new police in England. By 1822, the year of its disbandment, there were 2326 men in the PPF, only a minority of whom were Catholic. Of the recruits who joined between 1816 and 1822, 16 per cent were Catholic.[9]

It was not until 1822, with the formation of the Irish Constabulary, that Ireland had its first country-wide police force. Opposition to the idea of a police force delayed the introduction of the force in some counties, and ensured that control of the force was localized. Each barony was to have a force of sixteen constables commanded by a chief constable, with an inspector general for each of the four provinces of Ireland. However, numbers expanded rapidly. By 1824, there were 214 chief constables, 1113 constables and 3465 sub-constables;[10] manpower expanded another 23 per cent by 1830. The number of Catholics increased in parallel, ranging from 25 per cent in Connaught to 39 per cent in Munster.[11]

The centralization which was resisted in 1822 was recognised as a necessity by 1836, when a single force was established, save for the cities of Dublin, Belfast and Derry. The force was controlled from Dublin Castle, the seat of British power in Ireland, and under the authority of one inspector general, an ex-military commander from Manchester, James Shaw-Kennedy.[12] Along with the centralization of control and authority, the reorganization effected a strict disciplinary code, along the lines of the British Army. The army also provided the model for police uniforms. The training centre in Phoenix Park, home of the Lord Lieutenant in Dublin, was opened in 1839, and great emphasis in training was laid on drill, weapon handling, and military-style deportment and dress.

Over time, Phoenix Park became famed for the quality of its recruits, and its spartan conditions. Until 1908 there were only three baths for 500 recruits, and straw bedding was being used right up to disbandment in 1922, but the training itself was considered ideal. The British government eventually insisted that all commissioned officers in colonial forces be trained in Dublin before serving in distant parts of the empire. It was not just the colonies that received the products of Phoenix Park, for Steedman shows that of 24 chief constables appointed to English forces between 1856 and 1880, 11 had served in the RIC,[13] which is the exact reversal of the background required in law of the RUC's chief officer.

Ironically, while a background in a police force such as the RIC was considered suitable for other police forces, the RIC itself tended to be placed in the charge of ex-army officers. By the time he wrote his history of the RIC in 1869, Curtis, who was also a county inspector in the force, complained of the tendency to use the military as the model for the professionalization of the police in Ireland, and the associated habit of appointing ex-servicemen to senior positions in the RIC.[14] He poked fun at policemen who tripped over their swords at every step.[15] These complaints were echoed by magistrates and members of the public,[16] although the inspector general published a pamphlet denying 'military mania'; he resigned the following year. And as the century bore on, the RIC became more like a civil police force, developing a strong service function in the community, although, as Palmer illustrates, the RIC never completely shed its original role as a colonial police imposing force on an alien populace.[17]

As one measure of the eventual integration of the police into the local community, policemen often received testimonials upon their retirement, full of eulogies, and a large gratuity as a more material expression of affection.[18] This process of normalization in police-community relations was reinforced by the deliberate policy of minimizing transferals, so that policemen spent long periods in the same community, developing immense local knowledge useful in policing but along with it also continuity, familiarity and respect from the local population. As a result of this social integration, policemen came to enjoy a position of high regard, especially prior to the escalation in political violence after the 1916 Easter Rising. This was purposely cultivated by the police authorities. The 1837 Code of Conduct laid down that constables (who in 1883 became called sergeants) should be 'men respected by the people and obtain the good opinion of the gentry', while sub-constables (later becoming constables) were expected to be of high educational skill and ensure the 'general improvement of [their] mind'.[19]

This level of education was well above that of the local population and, in conjunction with the priest, policemen often provided the only source of reading and numeracy skills in the parish, although this was less so as educational provision improved over time. But policemen often read and composed people's letters, did the accounts for shopkeepers, and completed various official forms for members of the public. They regularly attended social events, and the presence of the local sergeant graced most important gatherings in rural communities. This is a good illustration of the benign mode of policing adopted by the RIC in many parts of Ireland towards the end of the nineteenth century. There were strict instructions laid down within police regulations about maintaining this standing within the community. Policemen were forbidden to marry until after seven years service in order to accumulate sufficient worldly wealth to maintain a high standard of living after marriage, and the bride was vetted. Policemen and their wives were prevented from engaging in many forms of trade; wives could be dressmakers but not employ apprentices. They were allowed to keep animals at home but not for profit and were prevented from selling produce or to take lodgers.

Over time, therefore, the RIC began to be seen as an indigenous police force and was able to successfully recruit from amongst the local population. At the time of the reorganization in 1836, the constabulary had a manpower of 10,000 men, rising by another five hundred in the next twenty years.[20] The improvement in relations with the community, and the paucity of employment in rural Ireland, influenced recruitment patterns, leading to the employment of increasing numbers from the local Catholic population. In 1836, two-thirds of new recruits were Catholic, and in 1842, 54 per cent of all constables were Catholic, rising to 76 per cent in 1880.[21] By 1913, 86 per cent of the recruits that year were Catholic, and 98 per cent were Irish born.[22] However, the officer class was still predominantly Protestant, many from English public schools who were recruited under an officer cadet scheme. Cadets were being recruited up until 1921, but complaints from within the force, first voiced in the last third of the nineteenth century, led to a growing number of promotions from the ranks. The 1866 commission on the RIC recommended raising appointments from the ranks from one in six to one in four; which had been done by 1883. The ratio was one in two by 1895. This inevitably increased the proportion of Catholic officers, but it never reached a level representative of their number in the ranks. By 1920, only 40 per cent of officers were Catholic,[23] although the force at this time had its first Catholic inspector general.

The life style of officers reflected their privileged Anglo-Irish, Protestant, and military background. Garrow-Green, from this tradition himself and a district inspector in the RIC, evokes this life style in his account of the force.[24] Officers from the cadet scheme had difficulty in comprehending the local peasantry, took police duties very casually, relying on their head constable (where many Catholics in the force ended up after promotion), and led a relaxed life attending theatres, tennis parties, hunting, shooting, and balls hosted by the gentry. Officers who liked the country life and who happened to be stationed in areas where the old county families survived, could lead a typically colonial life. But some officers in the West of Ireland found life very desolate and isolated. In evidence to the 1914 government enquiry on RIC pay and conditions, an officer in County Mayo said of the area, 'it is not a desirable place for a district inspector as there is very little society for him in it, and the country is poor and [has] no hunting grounds'.[25] Complaints were made about the change in the gun laws which no longer made it an offence for locals to carry arms, which had deleterious consequences for the quality of the game shooting. According to a partly-fictional account which features the exploits of officer Blake, an expensive and privileged life style persisted in some areas up to 1921;[26] during May 1920, for example, a tennis party was ambushed in County Galway in which a district inspector, among others, was killed, with only a relative of Sir William Gregory surviving.

In the early part of the nineteenth century, the police were a paramilitary organization divorced from the local population, whose purpose was to impose the rule of the Crown. The agrarian disputes and Catholic protests which followed from colonial rule, and in which the police became heavily involved, were often bloody and violent. Between the years 1824 and 1844, for example, four peasants were killed in clashes with the police for every policeman.[27] This explains why Ireland was more heavily policed per head of population than England at this time. However, in the 1880s, though popular support for the police was low, the death-toll was far below that of the 1830s. By 1914 a government report revealed that arms were carried only on ceremonial occasions and used merely in drill. Thus, while the RIC evokes the imagery of violence and force, whether in evicting tenant farmers or quelling popular protests, towards the end of the century duties were varied and often less controversial.

Policemen were responsible to collecting agricultural statistics, checking the sale of food and drink, estimating the size of the potato crop, helping the coastguard in protecting wrecks from looting, escorting patients to asylums, maintaining order at election polls, looking for poteen, checking lighting on carts and bicycles, preventing animals wandering onto public highways and cycling on footpaths, taking note of speeches at political meetings, preventing wakes for people who had died of infectious diseases, and arresting beggars and vagrants. The number of books and returns increased through the years until policemen were dealing with 29 official records by 1913,[28] ranging from weights and measures, and agriculture and food, to various internal reports, covering cycling allowances to crime statistics. The Dublin Metropolitan Police (a separate force from the RIC) were required in 1913 to keep the following records, among others: occurrence book (entry of incidents reported to the police), beat book (record of constables' tours of duty), bail book, prisoners book, habitual drunkards book, lost property book, military prisoners book, pedlars book, general dealers book, street cleaning by-law book, and a refused-charges book.[29]

By 1913 there were 1397 police stations in Ireland, the most heavily policed areas being in the South and West of the island (see Table 1).

Table 1: RIC Deployment by County

County	No. of stations	No. of men	Average pop. per policeman
Antrim	39	270	718[a]
Armagh	29	204	589
Carlow	16	82	442
Cavan	28	165	552
Clare	66	487	214
Cork	120	692	455[b]
Donegal	59	345	488
Down	44	279	732
Dublin	30	167	365[c]
Fermanagh	25	135	458
Galway	94	900	202
Kerry	59	349	458
Kildare	27	144	462
Kilkerry	40	218	344
King's	28	169	336
Leitrim	30	168	378
Limerick	53	299	349[d]
Londonderry	22	137	728[e]
Longford	17	112	391
Louth	19	126	505
Mayo	63	404	475
Meath	34	129	363
Monaghan	21	123	580
Queen's	23	130	420
Roscommon	39	282	333
Sligo	34	216	365
Tipperary	79	408	330
Tyrone	35	247	577
Waterford	30	175	322[f]
Westmeath	33	218	275
Wexford	38	185	552
Wicklow	26	151	462
Belfast	26	1263	306
Cork	11	174	440
Derry	5	105	388
Limerick	6	86	447
Waterford	6	69	398

Source: Minutes of the Committee of Inquiry into the Royal Irish Constabulary and the Dublin Metropolitan Police, with Appendices. HMSO. Cd. 7637. Appendix VIII.

Notes:
a: Excluding Belfast City Police
b: Excluding Cork City Police
c: Excluding the Dublin Metropolitan Police
d: Excluding Limerick City Police
e: Excluding Derry City Police
f: Excluding Waterford City Police

Despite the political quiescence in Ireland at this time, it remained more heavily policed than England. Belfast, for example, had a ratio of one policeman per 306 head of population in 1913, compared with 449 in Liverpool, 531 in Manchester, 610 in Bristol, 660 in Bradford and 683 in Newcastle.[30] But the RIC was not in a strong position. Morale among members was low as a result of disaffection over low pay and overwork. Some ranks (for example, Head Constable Major) had not received a pay increase since 1872, although the last major revision of pay was in 1883; there was a strike by policemen in Belfast in 1914 (there had also been a mutiny in 1882, prior to an earlier round of negotiations over pay). The force was under strength by 6.9 per cent,[31] recruitment was dropping, the standard of applicants falling, and the number of resignations rising. In the thirteen years up to 1913 there were 7783 resignations from the force; in 1901 there were 721 first class candidates entering the police, in 1914 the number was 19.[32]

In submissions to the 1914 government enquiry into RIC pay and working conditions, senior officers and constables alike pointed to the deterioration in the quality of candidates offering themselves for selection. The number of sons from farming families seeking employment in the RIC, the most stable source of recruitment, declined by 4 per cent between 1901 and 1913, whereas labourers rose by 125 per cent. Recruitment among teachers declined by 42 per cent and clerks by 46 per cent, while the number of recruits who listed their employment as gardeners, for example, increased by 200 per cent, grooms by 200 per cent, carpenters by 33.3 per cent, and postmen by 50 per cent.[33] There had even been a reduction in the number of recruits with fathers in the police, the age qualifications and the standards of entry for which were less strict. Thus in evidence before the committee of enquiry, the Commissioner of Police in Belfast said, 'now I have to be satisfied to take any man I can get'.[34] While urban areas were notoriously poor recruiting grounds for the RIC because of the availability of other well-paid employment, members from the rural areas repeated the sentiments. A county inspector from County Clare said of recruits, 'I won't say exactly that they come from a different social class, but we are not getting the pick of that class. In times past we got the best of those men'.[35] A constable from County Cork declared that recruits 'are so physically, intellectually and socially unfit that if they presented themselves ten years ago they would have been rejected outright'.[36] In these circumstances the government acceded to the request for a substantial pay increase, and was shortly to allow a regular review without the need for parliamentary legislation.

The government consented so readily because the worsening political situation in Ireland over home rule forced a greater reliance on the RIC, whose morale thus became important to the implementation of the state's authority in Ireland.[37] The army was at war in France and the police became the state's only line of defence in the renewed conflict over independence. The nationalist conflict eventually erupted in the 1916 Easter Rising, an event from which many commentators date the deterioration in the public image of the RIC,[38] although they have Nationalists primarily in mind. Fourteen policemen died in the Easter Rising, and 23 were injured, compared to a total casualty list of 500 dead and 2500 injured.[39] At the time of the rising, the strength of the force had declined by five thousand compared to 1883 (although this year represents something of a peak in the RIC's strength because of expansion during the land war); and while the 1914 committee of enquiry could congratulate the RIC on being 'well integrated' into the community, the force was never again to be so socially enmeshed and respected, although in some areas policing remained as benign as it had done for generations,[40] becoming militarized only after 1919.

The first police deaths of the civil war occurred on 21 January 1919, when two policemen were shot in County Tipperary, taken unawares by the renewed guerrilla campaign. Police stations were quickly transformed from homely, white-washed buildings into sandbagged, reinforced forts. In total, 425 policemen were to die and 725 injured until disbandment in 1922;[41] the peak occurred in March and April 1921 when 158 were killed during each month.[42] Nearly one in twelve members were injured and one in twenty killed in just over two years.[43] The anonymous author of *Tales of the RIC* claims that some members taken prisoner were tortured before being killed,[44] although this has to be doubted. A greater number of policemen were intimidated into resigning; the resignation rate in this period was double that for the decade from 1910-1919.[45] Members' families were intimidated, including children.[46] Potential recruits were also put under pressure to prevent them from joining, and many smaller, isolated stations were closed down because of their vulnerability to attack.[47] The boycott of the force, intended by Sinn Fein to restrict supplies and comfort to the RIC, further isolated many members where it was rigidly applied; in County Clare people were shot if they breached the boycott.[48]

For these reasons, the force has been portrayed as demoralized, disorganized, defeated and dejected.[49] This is something of an exaggeration for the sake of alliteration, for morale improved after pay rises in 1920, but there is no doubt that its most recent experience as a civil police force prevented the RIC being successfully remilitarized to cope with the onslaught. Thus, when the Ballinasloe police wrote to Sir John Anderson, a prominent British civil servant, on 30 August 1920, calling for the disbandment of the force, the major complaint was that the war situation made it impossible for them to discharge their duties as a civil police: 'we consider it is almost an impossibility to carry out our functions as a civil police force under the pressure of present circumstances. The strain on the force is so great...we are now useless as a civil police force. We as a body of men are not able to restore law and order'.[50]

The RIC was inadequate to the task of defeating a guerrilla campaign. By inclination it had become a civil police force. Its training, resources, and the psychological preparedness of its manpower equipped it poorly for transformation into a military machine, and its relations with the army were never good.[51] It was precisely because the older RIC men were not the brutal butchers and sadists portrayed by de Valera, that the intimidation and ostracism led to so many resignations and to the formation of the much more ruthless Black and Tans and Auxiliaries. The younger men who joined the RIC during the period of the civil war had a psychological preparedness for the job, and no experiences of policing in 'normal times' to make the contrast. But they were still policemen, trained in the way policemen had been for generations and subject to the strict disciplinary code of the force. The ex-soldiers recruited into the Black and Tans and Auxiliaries were employed for their skill in armaments and received little or no training in 'routine policing'. They were deemed to be already trained; it was their *modus operandi* as soldiers which was important, even if they had the dress of policemen, and sometimes not even that. Senior officers in the RIC tried to control recruitment in the Black and Tans, insisting on the police Code of Conduct being followed, and that great care be taken in selection.[52] The Auxiliaries, for example, were graded for discipline, pay and allowances as equivalent to sergeants in the RIC.[53] The inspector general was relieved of his post after complaining that many of these stipulations were not being followed.

There was a complete breakdown of law in some parts of Ireland during 1920, because of the unauthorized and officially encouraged retaliation by the security forces for atrocities against them. Opposition to the reprisals was voiced by politicians in Ireland and Westminster, including Lord Curzon, soon to be thought of as a possible prime minister, and his son-in-law, Sir Oswald Mosley. The actions of the Black and Tans caused the latter to leave the Conservative Party whip in the House of Commons. General Macready, the senior British Army officer in Ireland, and a former Commissioner of the Metropolitan Police, 'began to feel uneasy' at the behaviour of the Black and Tans, insisting that their uniforms be replaced so that their khaki would not lead to them being mistaken for soldiers.[54] The Black and Tans were not even averse to persecuting members of the RIC who had resigned or who were contemplating such,[55] and the Auxiliaries attacked members of the RIC.[56]

Relations between the RIC and the special forces, therefore, were not good. Shea describes his father's outrage at the conduct of the new recruits,[57] and a group of policemen in County Kerry, led by Jeremiah Mee, refused to co-operate with soldiers and resigned (although the mutineers included two Black and Tans).[58] The RIC's *Constabulary Gazette* wrote an editorial critical of the policy of recruiting policemen from among the English, and Fitzpatrick describes feelings between the respective security forces as constituting a separateness bordering on hostility.[59] There were several ugly incidents between Black and Tans and members of the conventional RIC. The latter adhered more strictly to the police Code of Conduct, which laid great emphasis upon religious and political impartiality in relations between members of the force (if not also in dealing with the public). For example, political and religious discussions were prohibited in barracks, religious tracts were confiscated (as commented upon by one of the ex-policemen in the following oral history), and policemen were supposed to be impartial in the conduct of their duties.

The neutrality evinced by many in the RIC, now taken for granted as the chief characteristic of a professional police force, was seen by some extremists as proof that the force was a fifth column for Sinn Fein. Leading Unionists in Ulster made allegations that many Catholic policemen were in league with the enemy and could not be trusted; a fear which led to there being a strict quota on the number of Catholic ex-RIC who could join the RUC. Suspicion was shared by some officers in the police (who would very likely have been Protestant), and one of the Volunteers interviewed by Griffith and O'Grady was an ex-policeman from the Dublin Metropolitan Police.[60] A county inspector in Limerick wrote a report to Dublin Castle to the effect that half his men were informers for Sinn Fein, the other half assassins;[61] but murderers for whom is unclear, because not all policemen refrained from engaging in reprisals. Farrell lists the reprisals undertaken by a squad of RIC in Belfast from 1920 until 1922.[62] Some policemen based in Ulster had an ambivalent attitude toward the criminal activities of Protestant organizations like the Ulster Special Constabulary and the Ulster Volunteer Force,[63] although the former was a legally constituted police force of sorts. The policy of reprisals was even given official endorsement by the inspector general, and notices posted in some areas warned of their prospect if attacks on the police persisted.[64]

Once the Dail ratified the Anglo-Irish Treaty and the British devolved power and responsibility to the provisional Irish government, the RIC was prepared for disbandment, although it had been expected for some time. By March 1922 the force was withdrawn from nineteen counties in the twenty-six county Irish state, with disband-ment centres established in each of the remaining counties, with the main centre in Gormanston, north of Dublin. Although the conflict with the police was at an end, old grudges were settled and many ex-policemen were attacked when back in civilian life. Kevin O'Higgins, arch Nationalist and a member of the newly independent Irish government, reminded Nationalists that joining the force had been the 'height of ambition' for many people, and some former members of the RIC joined the Garda and helped in training the new force.[65] However, the British government was forced to pay policemen with a permanent home in Ireland a disturbance allowance, arising from 'molestation and danger', for those who wanted to move themselves and their families to avoid the intimidation.[66] This encouraged some to join police forces in Palestine, Northern Ireland and in England. Pension entitlements for policemen were also problematic but even-tually conceded by the government.

Conclusion

The dominant portrayal of the RIC in the academic literature is as a colonial police force suppressing the Nationalist population.[67] The colonial model attributes to police forces the following features: a quasi-military appearance in equipment and training; an operational role designed to impose an alien political authority on the population rather than performance of a benign service function or conventional crime fighting, with the consequent merging of a policing role with civil, legal and political administration; non-integration with the community; and local recruitment into the ranks but an ethnically exclusive officer class.

This is indeed how the RIC began and ended up, but other writers stress how the force departed in significant ways from some of these characteristics during certain periods in the century of its existence. For example, policemen were not always divorced from the local community, before the civil war the force lost most of its military trappings and developed a service function and crime-fighting role,[68] which persisted in some areas up to disbandment, and the officer class was not entirely composed of aliens. This is not to say that the RIC followed the civil police model of English forces.[69] Rather, the RIC was caught in a conflict between both models, the outcome of which depended upon the wider political events, local circumstances and popular protests that pertained at the time. Its crime fighting and service functions, and the social integration of its members into the community were constrained by the association of the force with the state and by periodic popular protests, and its subsequent remilitarization and paramilitary role were restricted by the long experience of 'normal policing' in the quiescent periods during Ireland's struggle for independence. It is to this problem that the policemen in Ballinasloe referred in 1920 when they called for the disbandment of the RIC.[70] In this regard policing styles in Ireland have to be seen as reactive to broader national (and local) events rather than proactive; police forces are rarely independent actors, but closely influenced by their relationship with society and the state.[71]

CHAPTER 2

The oral history method

Introduction

Oral history is not a subject area of history, like economic, colonial or
political history, but a data collection technique which can be applied
to study any topic that is within the living memory of people. There is
no mystique about the method; people simply recall their life experiences and put their perspective on the events in which they partici-
pated. Thereby the analyst is able to augment and complement other
data sources, such as documents, archives and official records. It
cannot claim exclusivity, for oral history is not an alternative to the
usual historical sources but a supplement to them. The method
becomes hearsay if respondents are asked to report about the lives of
ancestors,[1] thus distinguishing oral history from the anthropological
collection of oral traditions. Hence oral history is restricted to the life
span of people, and thus mainly to topics and events in the twentieth
century.

   Although the technique has been used by historians for centuries,[2]
it first became popular in the 1940s, since when it has encroached into
other disciplines, such as social anthropology, political science and,
especially, sociology. In the latter, the technique merged with a longer
methodological tradition in which the use of oral sources, such as
indepth interviewing and the closely associated life history technique,
were legitimate and well established.[3] Indeed, oral history is one of
many meeting grounds between historians and sociologists, function-
ing to break down disciplinary boundaries between them,[4] although
the resistance of some historians to sociology enhances their distrust
of oral sources, as E.P. Thompson implied in reviewing an oral history
study by one of Britain's leading sociologists.[5] However, Paul Thompson, in the most notable programmatic statement in defence of
oral history, argues that the popularity of the method in sociology
during the 1950s and 1960s, which resulted in several excellent
studies, did much to confer legitimacy on the method among younger

historians, especially those concerned to document aspects of working class life and labour.[6]

The influence of sociology is evident in another sense. By nature sociologists concentrate their research on groups at the periphery of modern industrial society, a point on which it is criticized by supporters of the New Right, who claim there is an anti-capitalist bias in sociology. Goffman ascribed this tendency to the greater interest which these groups provoke rather than any resistance to private enterprise. He described sociology as prefering to study the standpoint of the 'hip outsider' than the 'dull insider', and it has analyzed numerous deviant sub-cultures and groups, focused on several unusual occupations, and documented the social worlds of those on the margins of society almost to the exclusion of 'dull insiders'.[7] In short, it offers a view from below. Oral history fits neatly into this because the method provides, as Thompson claims, a people's history, a more democratic approach to history.[8] By looking at events from the vantage point of those at the bottom of society, it charts the history of the unknown people who have not before been considered important; people who do not figure in documents and records – the soldiers rather than generals, the followers rather than leaders, the citizens rather than monarchs.

In enthusiastically appropriating oral history, younger historians also adopted sociology's standpoint, opening up to historians an array of new topics and groups formerly ignored by tradition-bound historians. Thus, historians now use oral history to contribute to such subject areas as labour history, women's history, and new aspects of social history such as the social life of children and the history of the family.[9] For this reason, there is a connection between oral history and socialism and feminism,[10] although the technique can be used to study conservative groups like former fascists.[11] However, as Samuel argues, this ideological bent is not inevitable, for oral history has been applied in some of the more orthodox subject areas within history, such as local history.[12] And one of the major contributions of oral history has been to add a new dimension to military history by documenting the ordinary soldier's account of battle. Oral history studies of this kind cover the distant past, such as the First World War,[13] and more recent conflicts, like the Vietnam War, the Falklands, and violence in Northern Ireland.[14] This genre also now includes studies of ordinary members of the police, such as Baker's work among American patrol officers.[15]

This is not to claim that oral history is without its detractors and does not have serious methodological limitations; its weaknesses need to be kept continually in mind when acclaiming its strengths.

Methodological strengths and weaknesses of oral history

The oral history method has not been well received by some historians, who belittle its contribution and are adamant in relying on
conventional data sources. The infamous remark by A.J.P. Taylor,
one of Britain's leading historians, is often quoted as evidence
of the dismissive attitude which oral history generates among some
people: 'in this matter I am an almost total sceptic... old men
drooling about their youth – no'. Some forms of oral history he
described as serving to mislead historians and are 'useless except for
atmosphere'.[16]

The complaints made against oral history are several. First, it is
supposed to be marginal because it is restricted to the modern sphere
and can only contribute to our understanding of twentieth-century
events. However, this does not impugn the validity and utility of the
perspective it provides on contemporary history. A more important
criticism is the claim that it is trivial. Because it is based on people's
recollections and reminiscences, the method ignores all those broader
processes and issues which do not penetrate people's minds and of
which they are ignorant. People can only recall from memory items
which originally impinge thereon, and structural processes and
changes which people have difficulty in perceiving or comprehending are thus left out of the analysis.

It is possible to respond to this criticism on two levels. The implica-
tion of this claim is that analysts are interested only in broader
structural processes and the ordinary features of life which can be
recalled are of little import. However, items which can be recalled by
people, because they impinged on their memory, may themselves be
important depending upon the topic of the research or the paucity of
information available on them. Moreover, the ordinariness which
people recall about their lives often provides a necessary counter-
weight to the drama that is going on around them and to which the
analyst's attention is naturally attracted. Historians can sometimes
over-dramatize a situation by ignoring how ordinary people experienced as mundane the momentous events in which they were involved. This is a striking feature of the way members of the modern
RUC react to the danger and threat they face.[17] In another sense, the
criticism assumes significance only if the method is not augmented by
other data sources which do take into purview the broader processes
often left out of people's comprehension. Oral sources become
unreliable when used in isolation or when not set in comparison with
data collected from other sources. Much might already be known
from other sources, leaving the ordinary person's perspective and
experiences as the last source of understanding to be tapped. This

gives the oral evidence an added interest and makes comparison with other data sources relatively easy. As the last chapter emphasized, the recollections of the surviving members of the RIC fit this case.

The most damning criticism levelled against oral history is that the data is methodologically suspect. The unreliability of oral data arises from several causes. These include poor memory, especially when involving elderly respondents, doubts about the veracity of the material because of systematic evasion, untruthfulness, *ex-post facto* glorification, or idealizations of the past, and unknown forms of bias deriving from the unrepresentativeness of the people from whom information is collected, often made worse by the small numbers involved. There are no easy responses to these weaknesses. However, none are unique to oral history. Conventional historical sources need to be treated with caution and investigated for their reliability, validity and veracity. In this respect A.J.P. Taylor is correct when he says that all sources are suspect.[18] But equal poverty is a bad argument in defence of method, and supporters of oral history have mounted a challenge against the charges.

Paul Thompson has argued at length against the criticism that failures in memory impugn oral history data.[19] Situationally specific props can be used to aid recall, such as old photographs and other memorabilia, and broad open-ended questions and supplementary prompts by a knowledgeable interviewer can help in the reconstruction of memory.[20] But stronger arguments are invoked, based on a new understanding of the nature of memory and the ease of recall of specific items locked therein. It is widely recognised that the long-term memory of the elderly is far more reliable and accurate than their short-term memory, such that they can often remember their youth better than the events of last week. It is this which gives impulse in psychiatry to the use of reminiscences for their therapeutic effect on the elderly.[21] The active process of reminiscence also instils in the elderly a sense of social worth, which derives from the interest shown in their experiences and knowledge;[22] an interest often lacking in immediate relatives who have heard the tales so many times before. Moreover, recall is easier for certain items. Past attitudes are recalled with less reliability than practical matters, and the degree of interest shown by the respondent in the item enhances accuracy.[23] Recurrent processes are better remembered than single incidents, but recall is improved for all items which have been consistently remembered over the years. Finally, the elderly routinely engage in what psychologists call a 'life review', in which towards the end of their life there is a sudden emergence of memories and the desire to remember, leading to a special candour which Thompson believes reduces distortion in the material.[24]

However, some respondents do engage in systematic evasion, denial, untruthfulness and self-glorification. This is a particular problem when social stigma attaches to them as people or to their former activities, so that their recall of the past is influenced by considerations of the present. Oral history research among former members of fascist movements shows that respondents engage in deliberate denial of the past,[25] or selective confrontation with the past in order to overcome pejorative evaluations of them as types of people.[26] Likewise, the use of oral sources to investigate persistently controversial aspects of political history requires analysts to disentangle the present from the past.[27] But other oral history research illustrates that people sometimes evade recalling personally disturbing or problematic incidents, are contradictory in what they say, can glorify their role and prominence in events, and provide uncritical idealizations or sanitized images of the past.[28] This is true for all sources which rely on people's self reports (such as interviewing, questionnaires, personal documents), but can be overcome by following the advice in the social science research methods literature. Oral historians should search for internal consistency in the narrative, cross-check details with other sources, weigh evidence against what is widely known to be true, and develop an innately critical attitude toward their data. Thus, members of the Black and Tans have to be disbelieved when they state that they never engaged in reprisals. It is also important to consider the dog that did not bark – the systematic avoidance of certain issues and deliberate silence on some matters. Such distortion should simply prompt the analyst to ponder the reason for the silence and evasion, rather than to question the reliability of the entire method.

Respondents in oral history research are often a self-selected group or some unrepresentative collection created by the accident of longevity or access. The small numbers involved can compound the lack of representativeness of respondents. But representativeness only becomes problematic if generalizations are to be made to a wider group beyond the people from whom the information was drawn. This can only be reliably done if the respondents form a random sample. While this is possible in some oral history research because of the large numbers of respondents available, most oral history studies rely for their relevance on the interest and knowledgeability of the respondents involved. Oral testimonies collected of a small number of survivors from those people who were actively involved in, and informed about, some past event or experience, can furnish important and interesting data. Their unrepresentativeness is irrelevant to the validity of what they report; it just prevents wider generalizations being made to other participants from whom information was not collected.

This is very much the situation with respect to the small band of survivors from the RIC who feature in this volume, for what they report cannot be taken as typical of policemen generally at this time without supporting evidence. Readers must also be aware of the tendency of elderly respondents to idealize the past.[29] Hence, for example, when some of the policemen talk in a seemingly casual manner about the danger from frequent IRA ambushes, the fear they felt at the time is being glossed over or evaded, thus creating a more sanitized image of the past than was the case in actuality.

Most of the supposed weaknesses of oral sources, therefore, are not insurmountable. But there are also positive qualities accruing to this form of data. Speech is a less restricted social skill than literacy and is not so affected by advancing age, so that those who find writing difficult may still be able to provide oral testimonies. This is true of categories like the elderly, who have lost the capacity to write through infirmity or failing eye sight, and non-literate groups who would otherwise be overlooked. This is one of the reasons why the use of the oral history method has expanded the range of people studied by social researchers and introduced new topics for study. Moreover, the contradictions that appear across people's oral testimonies should be seen as a positive benefit of oral history, for it emphasizes the multiplicity of standpoints and experiences that occur in reality. The complexity and ambiguity of the social world is sometimes lost in the summary portrayals and generalizations found in official records, documents and minutes.

Finally, the oral history method allows people the opportunity to offer interpretations of the past. The focus of the method here is not so much on obtaining an accurate representation of past events, but encouraging participants to display perspectives on the past. Given that these interpretations will be heavily influenced by the present, the method can be used in this way to give some purchase on understanding the present through the past, especially in contexts where there are political, ethical or practical constraints to the direct exploration of these issue in a contemporary setting. But it can be used less ingeniously to allow elderly people to look back on their life and to provide a review thereof. This is an important use of the method, where it merges with the life history technique,[30] if the person's life is deemed to be interesting, relevant or significant. It is also applicable where there is difficulty in obtaining ready access to a larger number of people for reasons of sensitivity, which is why the oral-history-as-life-history approach has been used most frequently to study deviants.[31]

The former policemen

Oral history research has been done using single respondents and large numbers, and the presentation of the evidence varies with each. In the latter case, the research is presented in the style of a collection of stories, none of which is very detailed or rich but whose worth arises from the general impressions that emerge as the individual stories are read together. In the former instance, the research is presented in the style of a single narrative of much greater depth and richness. Since the research reported here was based on fifteen individuals, the volume does not adopt the single narrative approach. Further, the oral testimonies have not been organized around individual case studies, with each person's story told in turn. Rather the oral evidence has been edited, disaggregated and organized around discrete themes, preventing each account being read in its entirety (with the exception of two members of the Black and Tans). While there are some disadvantages to this procedure, I have to admit a prejudice for the thematic approach.

However, to enable readers to place what is said in the context of the individual's broader life experiences, it is worthwhile providing here a brief biographical summary of the respondents. Where it is relevant in the text to understanding the account, I remind readers of some of the personal features of the respondent after identifying their name.

WILLIAM BRITTON:
Born in County Donegal, into a Protestant farming family. Joined the RIC in 1918, stationed in County Down. Joined the RUC after disbandment.

ERNEST BROOKES:
Born in County Londonderry, into a Protestant farming family. Joined the RIC in 1920, stationed in County Waterford. Joined the RUC after disbandment.

GEORGE CRAWFORD:
A Protestant, born in County Donegal. Father was a policeman. Joined the RIC in 1920, stationed in County Meath. Joined the RUC after disbandment.

ROBERT CROSSETT:
Born in Philadelphia to a Protestant family from County Londonderry. Father was a farmer. Joined the RIC in 1920. Stationed in County Tipperary. Joined the B Specials after disbandment.

WILLIAM DUNNE:
Born to a Catholic farming family in County Galway. Joined the RIC in 1917, stationed in County Kerry. Joined the RUC after disbandment.

JOHN FAILS:
A Protestant, born in County Limerick. Father was a policeman. Fought in the First World War, and joined the RIC as a Black and Tan in 1920, stationed in County Mayo. Joined the Palestine Police but not the RUC.

ROBERT FLIGHT:
Born in County Wicklow to a Protestant farming family. Joined the RIC in 1920, stationed in County Clare. Joined the RUC after disbandment.

PETER GALLAGHER:
Born into a Catholic farming family in County Fermanagh. Joined the RIC in 1918, stationed in County Sligo and Mayo. Did not join the RUC on disbandment.

JAMES GILMER:
A Protestant, born in County Monaghan. Father was a policeman. Joined the RIC in 1919. Stationed in County Londonderry. Joined the RUC after disbandment.

HUGH MCIVOR:
A Protestant born in County Antrim. Father was a policeman. Joined the force in 1920. Member of the quick-response Reserve Force, deployed throughout the areas of high conflict. Joined the RUC after disbandment.

ROSS MCMAHON:
Born into a Catholic farming family in County Fermanagh. Joined the RIC in 1919, stationed in Dublin city. Joined the RUC after disbandment.

THOMAS MCMENAMIN:
Catholic, born into a farming family in County Donegal. Served as a driver in County Mayo. Joined the RUC after disbandment.

WILLIAM STERRETT:
Protestant, born into a farming family in County Donegal. Joined the RIC in 1921, stationed in Queen's County (County Offaly). Joined the RUC after disbandment.

EDWARD SULLIVAN:
Protestant, born in County Clare. Father was a policeman. Joined the RIC in 1920, stationed in County Cork. Joined the RUC after disbandment.

JOSEPH THOMPSON:
Protestant farming background. Fought in the First World War. Joined the RIC as a Black and Tan in 1920. Stationed in King's County (County Offaly). Did not go to Palestine but eventually joined the RUC.

Interviews took place between 1987 and 1988 and were conducted at the home of the respondent. All were recorded on tape and transcribed afterwards. Interviews lasted between two and three hours, and some respondents were interviewed on more than one occasion. It is worth noting that more than half the respondents were Protestant, whereas the majority of members in the force as a whole were Catholic. Further, most now live in Northern Ireland, when most members at the time would have been from the South of Ireland. It is easy to explain these anomalies. Only the younger members who joined in the death throes of the force are still alive and available for study today, and in the latter stages the RIC tended to attract disproportionately more Protestants. Moreover, it was the younger members, with less pensionable service, who tended to move North to join the RUC. Because the respondents mostly joined the RIC during the civil war, the picture that emerges from their recollections is obviously different than that which would be the case with members who experienced normal policing in earlier periods.

Finally, the following transcription symbols are used in the text.
(RES)   Researcher speaking.
(...)   Unintelligible or untranscribed speech.
[...]   Reseacher's additional material.

CHAPTER 3

Recollections of policing in earlier periods

Memories of fathers in the police

CRAWFORD (father stationed in County Donegal).
He was a well-respected figure in Glencolumbkille. It was the local
sergeant then and the parish priest who ran the district (.....). After
going out on pension he became a Rural District Councillor until he
left to go back to County Donegal. Many of them turned to him for
advice and for the filling up of forms. And I do remember about 1911
[the act was passed on 1 August 1908] when the Old Age Pension
came out, it was only five shillings a week, and they came in scores to
my father to fill up the application forms to acquire a pension, I
remember that well. You had to be seventy years of age then and I do
remember him telling them that if their name wasn't on the 1871
Census they wouldn't be entitled to the pension at seventy. Relations
with the community were very good.
    The sergeant was in charge of the station. Generally in that station
the strength was one sergeant and four constables, and his job was to
run the station as it should be run, attend to the patrolling of the
district, see it was properly and adequately patrolled both by day and
by night, and that all complaints were attended to, promptly attended
to. There was very little crime, very little crime, the police time was
taken up principally by what they call 'still hunting' – running after
poteen makers. There was very, very little crime. No serious crime,
none, and the people all lived as good neighbours together.
    I remember one search for poteen. He was after seizing a worm, you
know the worm that's attached to the still. He found where the man
was working and arrested the man. When they were coming down
along the mountain he was wondering where the still was, you see, he
got the worm but he didn't get the still. Coming down the mountain
in under a shrubbery he saw the still lying, where it had been hidden
and he pointed it out to the man that had only been arrested. The man
says, 'well I couldn't tell you sergeant who throwed her in the bush'.

There was quite a lot of poteen making in Glencolumbkille. They called the whiskey that you bought in the shops the Parliament Whiskey, it wasn't strong enough for a lot of the men in those days. There were no evictions or problems over land in Glencolumbkille, but further down on the Donegal coast they had evictions at which my father had to attend. That was where there was a District Inspector was murdered, he was at those evictions [perhaps the death of District Inspector Martin, killed by a crowd while attempting to arrest Rev. McFadden at Gweedore in 1889]. The police didn't carry out any part of the evictions, they were only there to protect the bailiffs. The police weren't allowed to put their hands on anything, to remove anything from a house, or seize, simply to preserve the peace, that was their duty there and that's what they stuck to. He did not like the duty at all but he had no option.

They had guns in the Barracks, you see, each man had a carbine in the Barracks, probably, they had to do, you see, some Barracks were attacked in those days and they had it for the defence of Barracks, for carrying out important escort duty or something like that. Normally on patrol work all they carried was just the waist belt, handcuffs and baton. That's what my father carried, the waist belt, handcuffs and baton in the case, that was the equipment for those days.

FAILS (County Limerick).
He had to do his round of duty every day and at night, do patrols at night, things like that. Generally he nearly would give a fellow a cuff on the ear and not a word about it if it was something my father didn't think was worth bringing to court. They were always running to him. That was if anyone got into trouble; the first person they raced to was the local sergeant to see what he would think about it. I remember there was a sergeant in a place called Kilnabe in County Mayo and he was liked, well liked, because he never brought anyone in if he could help it. There was someone who came to him one day to ask his advice about something. This sergeant was a great man for big talk.

Father had to do a three hour patrol every morning. It depended on the gist of things, in some parts there was only four policemen anyway, and there'd be isolated places too; he generally had a bicycle to get around. There was no such thing as a car at that time. You see at that time too, everything had to be noted in a daybook, you see. The sergeant in charge had to patrol the men and see that their equipment was alright and that they knew this, that and the other in their area. I remember people running down to our house. 'Come up quick' they'd say, something like this, and although he didn't have to, he'd go up and maybe give him a crack or something like that with a stick. It's only a very odd one that would turn and they were generally younger, but older men and women, once they got the sergeant called out and brought up to settle the quarrel then it was alright; and of course, there was always the question of drink and the hours of drink. I mean, that was considered a pretty bad business to be drinking after hours, the police had very little option but to summon them. Well, of course, the less court cases you had the better from a climate point of view, but at the same time you couldn't over do it. You had to bring some cases up. Generally the publican was the one that was summoned more than anything else for supplying the drink.

He'd deal with anything because he had to make a report, you see, every day. Then people would call at the station and he'd have to answer any telephone queries. There weren't many telephones at that time in the out places, but he had to write all these things down and make a report. Then there were monthly reports and things like that. Then, of course, there was the court; it was once a month usually at these small places. There were a lot of the cases consisted of, say, breaking the licensing laws. On a Sunday you had to be have walked three miles before you could claim a drink. The local sergeant and sometimes a constable with him would go out; nearly every crossroads had a pub in it at that time.

There was much trouble over land. I remember that my father had to go up quite often on riot duty; they were always fighting and rioting, and he always had to take his lunch with him in a haversack – it was pretty rough. He just had to do it, mother always made him up four or five good, big sandwiches. They took it as a matter of course, that's their job, like.

GILMER (County Monaghan).
He was well respected, even Nationalists, they all respected him and spoke well to him. Indeed they looked to him for advice in everything because he was very well educated, he was preparing for the church before he went to the police; his father died and then he had to go to the police.

McIVOR (County Mayo, County Antrim).
The only crowd you [people in the police] were allowed to join was the Freemasonry, you could join it, but nothing else. But they [the RIC] were a very fine body of men. You see in the early days when my father was up in Ballina in County Mayo, the priest, the doctor, the JP and the sergeant all sat playing cards; the next night the traditional fiddlers come in, my father was a traditional fiddler and there was a big room and a wooden floor and they'd play all the old jigs and reels, and they'd dance the Irish dancing there. You see it were a pity it was ever destroyed and I couldn't say that it was a Protestant force that they

were attacking or hated; there were more Catholics than Protestants, a lot.

Well my father's was a small station [in County Antrim], just ticking over with one at that time, there was just the one there, my father. They burned us out. That was very early on, very early in 1920. My brother was home from the Flying Corps, and his uniform was there and they kicked it about and tore it and burnt it. Well, it [the station] was pretty sparse you know, there was a dayroom and a couple of bedrooms and the usual, a sort of a block of houses. He had a good relationship with the local community. The RIC were very popular till this evil got in among the Irish. It just shows you what Hitler did with the German population. But in early days, in my father's days, a Presbyterian hadn't as good a chance of promotion as a Roman Catholic or a Church of Ireland. I suppose they didn't recognise the Presbyterian.

Where he was stationed it was a small village. One time they issued a circular from Dublin Castle; the police were looking for a rise of pay, and they said for the RIC to look for a rise of pay was ridiculous because they are mainly recruited from the farming community and their people supplied them with butter, eggs and potatoes. They were going to have to keep them. That came from Headquarters in Dublin Castle. You see the attitude that was taken. You had £3.19s.6d I think then a week. But this was long before my time, but I remember that particular thing. Pay was starvation. It was hard to live on it. It would have been tight. There was five of us and I remember it was tight enough, only my mother was a good handler.

It made it difficult to keep up his position within the community. You see if a bill wasn't paid promptly they were at the door you see, and it wouldn't look good. Then you couldn't make friends too much with civilians, they always frowned on that so you couldn't be too friendly with them. They'd [the police authorities] think that you'd be soft on the law you see, if they'd commit an offence that you'd close your eyes to it. This made difficulties, you see I would liked to have joined the bands or something as a child seeing the bands going about, and you weren't allowed to do that.

He just did patrols in the area. There was about six hours a day broken up into patrol; just round to try to take the whole sub-district in at different times. Walk with a black thorn stick and talk as you go along. There was all sorts of things, cock fighting and the usual carry on, but they weren't really bad crimes, just unlicensed dogs and all that sort of thing, and drunk and disorderly. There would be fighting at the fairs. He retired just after I joined, thirty years on the force he had. He never got a job; he never bothered. There was only a certain sort of employment you could get. Well I suppose, you see, they [the RIC] were, latterly anyway, up against it very much and they [local employers] put their heads together and wouldn't employ them. You see, it was a semi-military force, the police, and that brought them into a terrible lot of trouble; my opinion would be that the army was the first defence. The Garda were right in that they wouldn't be armed.

My father's position was very good, very good. He was called 'sir' no matter where he went. 'Nice morning, sir', and all this. He was held in respect. Of course they lived a strict life too, nobody could point a finger at them. In Cullybackey [County Antrim] the idea was if a man got drunk he'd be put in a wheelbarrow and wheeled through the village. The station sergeant, this was before my father's time, he was a very dressy man and very correct man, but they got him into the pub, put drink into him, he didn't take drink as a rule, and they wheeled him up through the village, and he never did a day's good after it. He was so humiliated it did him harm. There's always some wags about every place you know, that do things. Oh aye, it was a good place to live in, you could hear the old blacksmith's forge going you see, the horses getting shoed and all. It was a real country life. A good place to live and the bands would come out on the twelfth of July and everybody would enjoy the band.

SULLIVAN (County Clare, County Galway).
It was a place called Carraghan in County Clare. The only problem they had, and that didn't occur very often, was people used to fall out over land and you might waken up some morning and find all your cattle driven off your lands. They might be taken away eight or nine miles into the unknown and left grazing on the side of the road or pushed into somebody's land. But they were nearly always able to recover them. His relations with the local community were very good, very good. The way they were down there at that time you never asked for anything. If you had a discussion with a neighbour and you said that you wanted potatoes dug, you wanted a garden tilled, they'd come and do it for you. You know they were that type, nice and friendly people, be delighted to do anything they could. The only thing, they used to continually fight over was land, you might get your walls knocked down; of course it was nearly all stone walls about the place, you'd find your cattle driven off, and if you were an object of contempt for people your house would be fired into. I must say, we never had the slightest bit of trouble of any kind with neighbours and we were the only Protestant family nearly in the county. The nearest to us was our clergyman and he was four miles from us. Now the way it was there, you had three or four cows and naturally enough you'd run up on calving time and the neighbours would supply you with milk, without asking even. They all knew about your cattle, they were breeding or otherwise, and they never gave the slightest hint but the milk was on your

doorstep in the morning. We had three cows and my mother used to keep fowl, geese, ducks, hens.

He never had anything serious. What might occur was a brawl among the locals on a fair day, but it was brushed over. Funny you mention poaching. In my first station, it was in County Cork, and the river Lee was nearly in our back yard, and at night time when the trout and salmon were breeding, we used to see gangs of men going up and down the river with the hay fork stuck in the sod of turf and it lit, paraffin oil poured on it, to make a torch. They went up and down the river with that and speared the salmon. We were confined to the station because the sergeant wouldn't allow us to go out and interfere with them. He wouldn't let us go out and we used to watch out the windows at them going up and down. I don't know what was his idea preventing us from going because we were only too anxious to go, but the courthouse was maybe two-and-a-half to three miles from us and by the time you'd gathered up witnesses and one thing another it would be all over.

I never heard of him dealing with poteen making. [After father moved] we were seventeen miles from Galway city and that borders on Connemara, and they used to make a lot of poteen in those days. A particular man would strap a keg on his back and wouldn't walk on the road, he would go through fields and hedges. He knew the country better than the locals did, and he used to supply them with the poteen. He was a very difficult man to catch.

No matter what took place around the country, such as an arrest, which was very, very rare, or a row over land, they'd all come to him [his father] to help them out with their problems. There was no such thing as going to the local magistrate, the sergeant or ex-sergeant was the better prop. When he said something they all agreed with it, it made life very pleasant for him. They wouldn't come into the house at times but they'd wait outside to see him. They would wait outside, then the next thing you might see was the door opening and a fellow would say, 'God bless all here'. That was the greeting. We used to get many people like that, they all wanted just a little bit of advice. My father was very, very well liked, never had the slightest fault to find with the neighbours. If we had a cow running dry, coming up on calving time, the milk would be found at the door for us; at least there'd be a can of milk left.

I never knew him to carry a firearm, unless on a special patrol for instance. The only kind of trouble he had to deal with was walls knocked down and cattle rustling, driving. They came in collision with the police but it wasn't planned same as it is now, and the police had no great difficulty in overcoming it. They might make an arrest or two. The trouble was nearly all land. Your people might have land that once belonged to me that would go back into maybe ancient history and I'd still spark over losing it. He was like myself, a Unionist, although he never gave expression to it. If he could stop it at all he would stop it, and often he was obeyed. The people weren't as aggravated as they are now, somehow or other, they were a different breed altogether.

Childhood recollections of policing

BRITTON (Protestant, born in County Donegal).
There was a station about a mile and a half or two miles from us, there was a sergeant and four constables. They were maybe a quarter of a mile or so from the nearest house. They had nothing to do; no crime, maybe a light on a bicycle, light on a cart or so. Well then there was poteen makers and that was their [the RIC's] principal job. It was a big area alright, but it wasn't very highly populated. They did occasionally come across poteen. You'd a half pint for a shilling. In Donegal you were near the sea and it wouldn't matter where you went they [the locals] buried it [poteen] in the sand hills. They buried the barrel of wash in the sand hills, covered it over and you could walk over it a dozen times. Well then they hid the still in some out-of-the-way place too. There was a small island and they used to go out and take the poteen and all the equipment out there on a boat and make a still out there. They weren't frightened of the police or anything.
   I could tell you a story about an island, Arran Island off the coast of Galway. There was a sergant and four men on it. The Norwegian fishing boats called at this island and they got in touch with the local sergeant and he went away with the boats to Norway and stopped there, and come back in two weeks' time. The books were all filled up. Nobody knew. The books were all filled up. There's a ferry boat run from the mainland on to the island and when there's a [RIC] officer on the boat, the captain had a signal with the horn, he gives two or three toots of the horn or whatever arrangement there was. Well then, they got time to get the men out on patrol or something.

BROOKES (Protestant, County Londonderry).
Maghera and Magherafelt were the only two police stations near us. About four men to either station. You would hardly ever see a policeman, hardly ever see one unless you were in the like of Maghera or Tullaghmore, you run across them that way, that's all. We feared them. I went to serve my time as a joiner and there was a policeman come in one day and he came up to me he had us shaking. He was later kidnapped. We were frightened of him.

The sergeant in the local station was a perfect man, a very, very, fine man. So was his wife and all the family too. He was well respected. He was a man that could go anywhere, you know, pleasant and likable.

CROSSETT (Protestant, County Londonderry).
There was several in the area. They used to have you up for petty things, no light on your bicycle and, ah, they were all very friendly and mixed well. There was Reilly the man that helped me get on the police here, a Roman Catholic. The police were good, they used to come out and my mother was alone you know, and this meningitis was an infection and there was bedclothes. It was a pathetic time for they had to burn the clothes you know, burn up everything, the police would come out to sort of supervise and they were very sympathetic too. They were all good and nobody held any spite against them till the Easter Week 1916. Then Carson come as our leader and a lot of them would tell you that he was a great fellow, but some of us Liberals, like, would have went into the Free State. We were used to Dublin, but anyway, there began to be frictions crop up.

DUNNE (Catholic, County Galway).
In County Galway policemen were very respected men, oh, yes. In fact they were called gentlemen. Oh, they were. Oh, I loved them, oh, they were very well respected, they were. For instance, if you wanted advice over anything, even law, you know, that sort of thing, you'd always go the police. In fact it was said that the parish priest and the sergeant were the guardians of the parish, that was the usual saying at the time, so they were very well respected. It was only a couple of years after my time [on the force], in 1921 that they didn't respect you then. But the time I joined it was grand.

FLIGHT (Protestant, County Wicklow).
The station wasn't near but it was in the town. Of course it was a large building too, very large building, it was enclosed with a big wall. They were a fine lot of police and at that time I don't think there was any young blood in the Barrack. The police were very much respected at that time. They were important people within the community, and then it gradually died away, you see, the grip that they had on the people. And then, of course, the rebellion started in 1916 and from that on things went from bad to worse.

GALLAGHER (Catholic, County Fermanagh).
In Boho, there was no trouble at all. There was no trouble till 1920. There was a police barracks up the road. There wouldn't be more than three or four in it at any time. They'd be out patrolling just the same, there wasn't much change in the duties from I was young until I left.

McMENAMIN (Catholic, County Donegal).
The District Inspector there, I remember, I used to feed his horse for
him. It was him who used to be mad for me to join the police. I don't
know, they used to get commended or something if they could get
good recruits, you know. The police were alright. They used to look
after people's cattle to protect them from the evicted tenants, you had
to protect them going into fairs and out of fairs and all, protect the
landlord, and the men that worked for them and all. Evicted tenants
used to try to drive cattle all over the country. The police were more
or less on the side of the poor, didn't abuse them in any way, they were
more or less on the side of the poor. They got fair play anyway to say
the least, there was no beating them down, batoning them or anything
like that, though some of the old landlords were quite good, you
know. There was some bloody rotten bad, so there was. Oh there was
some of them, if the farmer or the small farmer couldn't pay the rent,
if they had a good looking daughter she was taken instead of the rent
for an immoral purpose. Daughters would have to for to save the
farmer from getting put out and all. Oh aye there were a few of them
in Ireland like that. There was one up in my county, as a matter of fact,
they murdered him, they murdered the landlord there [possibly
refers to Lord Leitrim, murdered in 1878 near Milford in County
Donegal]. You see at that particular time too if you were in a house and
if you got a bigger window put in, the windows were all wide inside and
they went out till there was only a small pane, for you were taxed on
the light. Or if you built a wee bit of a wall in front of the house and
whitewashed it they put up your rates, the landlords did.

Constables weren't against the landlord in any way but they were
fair, I'd say they were more in sympathy with the poor ones than the
big fellows. You see, you could have been a farmer then and you had
a cornstack and you couldn't thresh it, you had to get permission and
maybe the corn was removed. You had to get permission, or if you had
seed the landlord would have seized it. Ah it was bad, it was a poor
country.

STERRETT (Protestant, County Donegal).
Police were very friendly, very friendly, they used to come down to our
house, and when my brother would be home on holidays they'd a
come down and played cards see, they used to come down and be
welcome. But mind you the old sergeant was crafty, he got the news
of the whole county. For goodness sake, when I was little if you saw a
policeman you run. There was one man there, he was very fond of the
booze, very fond of the whiskey, he could drink a ten glass bottle and
walk away. I was stationed with him as a sergeant in the RUC in Belfast,
so he knew all my place and we used to have great yarns.

They used to walk out and just go out and do a little bit of sheep dipping, unlicensed dogs, see if your gun had a certificate, all this carry on; they were all very friendly, no trouble, there was no trouble see, until 'the troubles' started. Oh they were well thought of, the ones in our area were all very nice, all very nice. Of course that was their idea to keep friendly with you because that's how they got their information.

CHAPTER 4

Childhood in rural Ireland and entry into the force

BRITTON

I was a native of Donegal, the most northerly point of Ireland, Malin Head. You see at that time, a policeman's son could join when he was 18. The ordinary clodhopper, you may say, had to wait till he was 19. What the discrimination was I don't know. My father had a small farm, the farms in Donegal that time were seldom large. I went in [the police] for a job, nothing else, but from when I was very small I always wanted to be a policeman. Well, in Donegal there's nothing but farming and small farms at that, and a lot of them had big families and the only thing if you didn't join the police you went to America. Very few went into the army. There was ten in the family, but the two eldest died when they were young. I never saw them at all. I understand they died of diptheria. We had the doctor alright but he didn't know what was wrong with them. Two stayed on the farm, both dead now too, and then there's two went to America, two brothers went to America and two sisters married, had homes of their own.

I had a hard life. Once you got say about ten, you were out into the fields, hoeing potatoes, cutting turnips and pulling weeds, and then you had to cut turf, you had to start and look after the turf, that would be about May. You had to clean out the stables and byres and things like that. You had to have a little of each, we'd usually two horses and three cows, then other animals, we had sheep, we'd about ten or twelve sheep, then you had fowl, a lot of hens and the hens were supposed to keep the house going. You'd sell the eggs, and one time I remember, well I suppose they were small, sixpence a dozen for eggs. You had about three months in the winter time at school. It was a hard life because you were working all the time, you never got any money, you might get a half crown going to a dance, to market, a fair or something. Everyone had to make whatever money there was off the farm. It was happy enough because at that time you knew no better. You just had to work and that was that, you were expected to.

33

When them that were in the police [from the local area] come home and they'd be telling great yarns about the work in the police, I listened to every word of this. To join the police, that was my ambition from a very small boy. I did not like working on the farm, not at that time, as I got older I liked it better. There was a good few [from the village in the RIC], a good few. I mean to say there was nothing else here. There was very little, there was no public works at all. You might say for any public work you'd have to go to Derry. Well then there was very little transport. There was a railway station, what they call the Londonderry and Lough Swilly Railway, although later on they had buses.

I joined [the RIC] during the war, although the war finished shortly. The war finished when I was in the Depot in Dublin. I joined the army first. I wrote away at the outbreak. Well, I wasn't eighteen at the time and the parents claimed me off, so I had to give an undertaking to my mother not to do it again. There was about three or four Protestants joined the army. A chap I went to school with, went to church with too, he joined the Inniskillings but he was wounded in France and lost a leg. The RIC was the next best thing.

It was the time of the Home Rule Bill and there seemed to be very little social life at that time. That's the time they were drilling for the Ulster Volunteers, and then there was the Nationalists. Well there was no Ulster Volunteers in my part of the country because there were very few Protestants compared to Roman Catholics. As a Protestant I never felt in danger or anything or got beat up or anything. You talked to your neighbours and went about with them. Except, I mean you went to separate churches but that was it. You drank with them if you were that way inclined and had the money. There was a lot of them used to go to Scotland, you see, for the harvest, as labourers. Anybody went. They stopped then till the potatoes were done, and then they came back and whatever money they had they usually drank it.

BROOKES
I was born in Ballyhorn, Tobermore, County Londonderry. I was only three years old when my father died and my mother was left with five of a family, the youngest was six weeks old. He was a farmer and he got pneumonia, and at that time they couldn't do much for it. He lived closed up in a room just, and eventually he died. My mother reared us all up till I went away, when I was about nineteen, to Belfast. Life was hard. There was no pension, nothing at all. No widow's pension, no old age pension. She kept the farm. She let the land, she kept a field for a cow, a wee field for potatoes and a field of corn. We sent the corn away to the mill and got it ground into oatmeal, and we had oatmeal porridge, home made bread on the griddle just over an open fire.

They were very lean times then. Friendly neighbours, they were. If we were short of milk the neighbours always helped us out. I went to school up to twelve; two miles to walk there and two back again. I was fairly good at maths and things like that. There were wet days when we didn't go and maybe missed a subject, and the teacher was starting some new subject and you didn't get in on it at the start, well, you were lost. We lost a lot of time on wet days, on winter days and we didn't just get a chance, you know, not what like they have today.

I didn't stay too long [on the farm]. I went to Belfast and got a job in Belfast and from there I joined the RIC in 1920. The joinery job was very slow and it would be a long time before I could work on my own, you know. You got no money at all. You got your food just, that's all, no money. My mother, two sisters and a brother went to Canada, but Belfast was quiet then, no trouble, and you could have went anywhere, not like today. I thought it extraordinary, the trams, holding on to the trams, going on and off the trams and so on. Then I took a notion I would join the RIC. I thought there was a wee bit more money in it. You started with three pounds ten a week. I thought it would be a nicer job.

CRAWFORD
I was was born in Glencolumbkille, County Donegal. There were eleven in the family and I was born on the second day of October 1898. My father was a sergeant in the RIC in Glencolumbkille, that's how I came to be born there. Well, my father was born on 15 August 1855 and he joined the RIC on 7 June 1875, he was not twenty when he joined. He was a sergeant in Glencolumbkille and he was then transferred to Sligo, to a place called Clogher in the county of Sligo, where he finished up and retired. My father was a farmer's son from County Monaghan and after leaving the police in Sligo he returned to Glencolumbkille, where he was appointed as the Sub-Postmaster, where he remained for a good number of years. He eventually bought a farm in his own native county in Monaghan. It was from there I joined the police.

My childhood was very pleasant, certainly, there was everything, people were getting on well together then and I enjoyed my life. Life was pretty hard, people had to work harder than they do now for to gain a livelihood, but to take it all round life was pleasant enough. Father laid a great emphasis upon education. The first school I attended was taught by a schoolmistress and when I came to about twelve years of age my father thought she hadn't sufficient control over me and he sent me to where there was a schoolmaster, in a Catholic school in Glencolumbkille. There I acquired whatever education I have with a smattering of the Irish language which I learnt there in school. We were a Protestant family but my father thought at that age I would be better to go under a schoolmaster who would have more control over me. I think probably he was right. I enjoyed school, played football along with the lads then, it used to be nearly always Gaelic football in that part of the country at that time. I enjoyed it, every day of it. The parish of Glencolumbkille was mostly Roman Catholic. There were little communities of Protestants here and there. We mixed with them [Catholics] and went to all the sports meetings, wakes and funerals, there was no difference made in those days over religion.

(RES) So you had no problem in growing up as the son of a policeman?

None whatever, none whatsoever.

CROSSETT
I was born in Philadelphia in the USA. My uncle Bob was the farmer here [County Londonderry]. There were two boys, my father went to Philadelphia and the other boy, uncle Bob, was on the farm. He fell off a horse, hurt his head and he died. Then my father thought he'd go home and take over the farm. That's what brought us home and we were all reared on the farm. I was about two. There was nine of us altogether. We were all tearing round and coming along wonderful, I had left school, just fourteen, and my father took meningitis and died. My mother was English born and didn't know much about farming. We had a tough enough time you know, but we got on. There was nine of us and every one went into business for themselves, we were all very lucky, hard working and progressive.

There was no talk about religion. The Roman Catholics they celebrated Hibernians' Day, and the Orangemen, our people, used to lend them a drum and flutes, you know. We mixed, we were very friendly with our neighbours and all, there was no difference till Carson come on the scene and then the Home Rule Bill didn't go through. My grandfather was a Liberal and we were all Liberals, I suppose, there was no talk about Unionist or anything else at that time. I still visit my old neighbours [Roman Catholic] and they still visit here. If it was a good evening and you had your hay pretty well ready for putting in the ruck, do you see, well my neighbour, may be he wasn't as far forward, then, of course, you helped him when you got a chance. We all used to work and help each other, used to have dances at night and one thing and another in the neighbour houses.

Before I had turned fourteen, I believe, I said I was leaving and I went away to a neighbouring farmer and asked him would he give me a job. He said he would surely and I started to work for him. It brought in a few shillings for my mother as well, you see. One of the farmer's brothers had a grocery shop in Magherafelt, and then he asked me to go in and drive the grocery cart. It was just a horse and cart. I went in there, bettered my position, I was getting more money and it was more, well a better job. Well I was working there and Head Constable Reilly – I was a brave, big fellow, plenty of flesh on me – and he says, 'you should join the police, a big fellow like you, join the police'. Says I, 'I was born in America and I haven't my birth certificate and I mightn't be the age at all'. 'Ah', he says, 'we'll soon fix that up'. He drew up an age and signed it, also my mother. We were all great friends but this trouble had started, you see, and they were fighting for the liberty of Ireland, you see, but he helped me, got me on and away I went.

I wasn't very smart, I wasn't well educated, I was about the worst in the form like, but I had a great flow of language and I was able to talk to anybody, you know, and with one thing and another I got through the exams and went to Derry city. I stood the final exam and got sworn in and got sent on to Dublin. I was about the biggest dunce ever, you know, I learned nothing at school, but they were pretty hard. I remember the man in Derry whoever he was, he was a Head Constable or something, he was giving me the dictation, you know, and I was writing it out, then I had the arithmetic to do. Says he, 'you're not very good but you're a good talker, I think you'll get through'. I was game you know. That was a powerful step up for me [to join the police], for a poor fellow like me, you see. Oh, I was anxious, but I many a time wondered why he [Reilly] went to all the trouble he did you know, for somebody that he had no connection with like, but he done it.

DUNNE

I was born on 10 October 1896 in Tuam, County Galway. I was the eighth child of a family of nine children consisting of four boys and five girls. I was a farmer's son and I worked on a farm after leaving school. I joined the RIC on 17 April, 1917 and my regulation number was 69081. Times were hard and labour was scarce, and of course money was scarce; there was no other employment. All the family went off, most of them, to America and I decided with a chum of mine to join the RIC.

I went to a National School. I was fairly good. You needed to be to get into the RIC, especially those years of the war; a big lot of the fellows from the West [of Ireland] used to go to England, labouring men, and conscription was coming in England and a lot of them didn't go [to England] and they joined the police. There was fifty-five that went with me to the Depot to be examined and out of the fifty only twenty-five were taken, less than half. There was a big number of men at the time and they were rejecting them for next to nothing, you had to be perfect. Well, a chum of mine, a next door neighbour of mine, another farmer's son, he joined the RIC and I went off with him. There was another brother on the farm, and, anyhow, in that locality a big crowd of fellows joined. I think eight of us joined the police in that townland.

FLIGHT

I was born in Arklow, County Wicklow, 1897. A family of nine. My father was a small farmer. It was a tough life for him for he got injured early in life and he was a cripple for the remainder of his life. Farming was very difficult. As the eldest son a lot fell back on me. There was just two boys in the family, of course the other, the brother, he did his bit too. He was a right good worker. I do remember them as very hard days. Money was scarce and you had to work very hard for to make a living.

I didn't get very much schooling. Working on the farm was a bit of a drawback. I was not extra bright. I didn't get the time, like, for to educate myself. When I left school there was nothing for it only get stuck in the farm, and then I got a job in the post office. There wasn't enough finance to keep the farm going and I held on to the post office job till I joined the police. I joined the RIC on 29 March 1920. The money was better, and then there were a couple of ex-policemen's sons joining and I suppose I got in with them. I never thought of trouble.

GALLAGHER

I joined the RIC on 2 April 1918. I was twenty-two. It was tough to get on, you know, those days. A couple of years after anyone would nearly get on but not when I was there; you needed education, physical and medical, and education was the simplist. If you were a fairly good sixth form scholar in my time at the National School, you went through first class. I had an uncle on the police. Until 1918 I was knocking about and getting an odd shilling here and there. Money was scarce, a shilling a day was all the best of them had, and they hadn't it every day. Money was scarce though.

I was born in Boho [County Fermanagh]. My father was a farmer. Life was tough growing up, old farmers hadn't much money. Where I come from in Boho it was all cut away bog and things. They had to put in a lot of crop. It was moss, horses would have been no good, you had to do it with a spade and shovel. You had to work hard to make a living. When I came back [after leaving the RIC] I started the farming again, I could have stayed on the RUC but I didn't. There was seven or eight of us in the family. They were difficult times. I don't know if there is any of the family alive or not. There may be one was out in America, I wouldn't know. There's only one, if there is any. I would say there wasn't a family that nearly had someone in America round here at that time. Emigration was easier got over than now. Of course, you always wanted someone to claim you when you went to America, if you hadn't they wouldn't let you in.

I just sort of wanted to get a job. There was nothing else. Money was very scarce. I was average at school just. I tell you it was the easiest exam [passing out from the RIC]. There was a whole lot of odd ones joined the RIC even before my time.

GILMER

I was born in Ballybay, County Monaghan. There was ten in the family and one died in infancy. My father was a sergeant in the RIC. When he retired he contested the election for Clerk of Petty Sessions. We had a farm at Bailieborough, and he was a sergeant in Carrickmacross, and he'd cycle back and forward to the farm, you know, when he would get a few hours off. There was forty acres of land. Eventually he took out an auctioneer's licence and he did a good trade in it. I had a fairly prosperous upbringing.

I was at a National School and then I went to Bailieborough Model for a while; it prepared them for training colleges and other colleges. Father put a great deal of emphasis upon getting his children educated. Then I joined the police in 1919 at twenty-three. I was turned down at first for measurements, my chest measurement, and I learned that they were getting a rise of pay then and they were turning down the recruits until they got the rise of pay. They told me they'd call me back again, at any rate, I went back and they passed me the next time. They told me to take exercises and my measurement increased, but I was really the measurement when I went the first time. I was on the farm and I thought of the police and I suppose a bit of excitement with it, the trouble was bad then; excitement.

McIVOR

My father was in the police. It was my father actually that put the notion in my head. He said there's something going to happen after this [Home Rule], the police would probably be done away with and some other force introduced, and if there's anything to be got out of it you might as well try. That's how I joined.

My father was on the police in County Antrim. As a matter of fact a big lot of my relations were on the police; my uncles and brother, and brother-in-law as far back as the time when they had about eight pence a day. Oh it was a good village, the people were all friendly and it was a nice place to live. There was some industry, there was a mill there and a good fishing river. My father used to fish there and when you were fishing the youngsters would come along and stand beside you, my father said never, never speak to them or say anything to them because if you do they'll stay with you and the next thing they're throwing stones into the river. My father was a a great fisherman. You'd ask him, 'what did you catch, did you catch many?' 'If I'd five more than the one I'm after I'd have six.' Oh yes, a good village, a good village. There was always plenty of employment in it and a lot of gentlemen's residences all about that area. Ah people high up in the world you know, and gentlemen farmers that had race horses and stocks of show cattle, and all that sort of thing. Gentlemen farmers you used to call them; and lovely acres of lovely woodland you know, landscape and good lands.

MCMAHON
I was born in Skendelly, Derrygonnelly. There was just three of us. Father was a farmer, he also worked in a public house the odd time in Enniskillen. I worked on the farm till I was about twenty years of age and then I went and joined the police.

MCMENAMIN
I joined on 30 April 1920, I wouldn't be 20 years of age then until 3 October 1920. I was born in Donegal. My father had farms, two farms there. There was a big family of us. I joined the police and the other brothers, two brothers, stayed at home on the farm. There were eight, six brothers and two girls. I had another brother on the police, he joined 1 January 1917, New Year's Day. I could've stayed on the farm because I was the ploughman and handled the horses and all. Then the eldest one of the family, the eldest brother, who was already on the RIC, I suppose he encouraged me to join. In our parts it was America, the army or the police. They joined the army too during the 1914-1918 war, a lot of them.

It was a good life, the best. Father's two farms were both good land, especially one of them. I was quite well off. There wasn't a big lot of money on the farm in those days, you know, because prices were very bad. You were always sure of plenty of food anyway. There was ones at that time in a poor way. My father had a job himself, for years he was a landlord [land agent] for one of the big fellows as they call them there, they had a big place outside of Drogheda, but they had another in Donegal. But my father had a job there, he looked after the whole place for them there and they had a few other men employed. He used to manage it. He left that job then and was full time on the farm, he also bought and sold cattle as well.

But generally speaking the life was great down there, you know. I didn't go to a secondary school I just went to the ordinary school till

I was fourteen. I had a great schoolmaster. He had eight brothers and seven of them were schoolmasters, and the other was a sergeant on the police in Downpatrick. He had two sisters and they were schoolteachers as well. The whole family were teachers; he was a BA too, and at that time very few of them had degrees. We had dances whenever the corn was saved. We grew flax too, that was worth about four hundred pound a ton weight in the 1914-18 war; they used it in the planes.

STERRETT

I was born in Donegal, a farmer's son. We were a big family, the most of them went to America, a brother and four sisters went to America, and two of the sisters were nurses in the City Hospital [Belfast]. I was on the farm but then I was good at figures so I got a job as a shop boy. A shilling a day, six days a week, no half-day. I stuck that for nearly a year, he [the shopkeeper] was alright but she was a tartar. She was a Scots woman, man the customers didn't like her. From the day he met her till the day he married her was twelve days, twelve days. The farm was only suitable for one, although my father wanted to leave me the farm, I was a good worker. Says I, 'no'. Well then I left the shop and I was home again for about two or three months when I applied for the RIC.

I'm a Protestant see and there wouldn't be many Protestants where I was you know, nearly all Roman Catholics. Although we were all very friendly see. As a matter of fact, another brother was home one time, he was out shooting and they come to raid the house, attacked it with guns, the IRA did, came to raid our house, and my mother was there. She thought they were going to take us away and she took meningitis and she was doing this when she was dying – 'keep them out, keep them out'. So anyway, this man come in the middle of the night and he said, 'you've a gun here and we want it'. We had the gun but we'd already handed it in, they advised anybody who had guns to hand them in to the Barracks. 'Yes', my father says, 'we had a gun alright but we handed in to the Barrack, we have no gun here now'. The one that spoke, they were all in disguise, this man says, 'I know this man, we'll take his word for it'. And away they went, didn't come in see, didn't come in for it was in the middle of the night. I remember them hammering the door. Oh we knew who they were, we knew who the most of them were; all neighbours nearly, all neighbours. Well they always took a stranger to lead them, a man from some other area, but we knew. [My brother who was in the RIC] was home, the time my mother died he come home; it was dangerous for him to come home. I remember that night when he was home and my mother died, two car loads stopped at the gate and they had a big conversation. My brother cleared off the next morning see. The Roman Catholics and

all, they all attended the funeral, neighbours as usual you know. He
went away the next morning.

SULLIVAN

I joined on the 30th April 1920. I was just reaching 19. I was born in
County Clare and my father was an ex-RIC man, and shortly after he
retired we moved into County Galway. He himself was a native of
County Galway and I suppose he wanted to get back to the old habits.
I was about eight or nine when I moved to County Galway. He was
stationed in a place called Carraghan, in County Clare, and we moved
into a place called Tullagh and lived in a thatched cottage. He never,
you know, went in for any kind of publicity and he lived a quiet life,
he worked hard and there was seven of us in the family, and the
parents of course made nine.

As a matter of fact I was delighted with the idea of joining the police.
We were eager just for work and couldn't get any. There was nothing.
There was either the police or go to school. I attended the ordinary
National School, it was Roman Catholic, there was nothing else for us.
There was no Protestant school. After leaving school the only thing
you might get in would be a shop assistant, and that would be about
maybe less than half-a-crown a week.

As I say, I started in the National School and we moved. My mother
got a job, but she didn't like it, caretaker in a school in Elphin in
County Roscommon. We were there for about two years. My father
[who was now retired] found it difficult to make up his home. He
retired somewhere about 1907 or 8, but he was getting old. As I was
saying, my mother got a job as a school caretaker in Elphin in County
Roscommon. It was a Protestant school and it was a long way from her
home, and my father found it very difficult. She was absent from home
and there was three girls there [at home] and they needed a bit of
attention now and again. I went to Elphin grammar school, that was
the Protestant school, for about two years with my mother there, and
then we had to go home because the expenses were far too heavy.

Well when I came home from grammar school I was itching to get
away. The first opportunity I got I took it, and went into the police
station in Gort in County Galway. I passed my exams flying, and on the
30 April 1920 I passed my exam in Galway. I was put on the train for
Dublin and sworn in. I used to hear so many funny stories about the
trams [in Dublin]. If you were near any of the old Dublin tramway men
they used to tell you stories about a recruit who got on a tram one day
and was watching the people going upstairs and was a bit curious. He
said to the conductor, 'mister is there anything extra to get up in the
loft?' You heard stories and yarns like that, made you laugh and enjoy
the run.

We knew the end [for the RIC] was coming, it was only just waiting to get the blow. We knew quite well it was going to haggle out but there was nothing else to do. It was either that or join the army and I didn't want that. A brother joined the RIC before me and the other one joined the Civic Guards.

CHAPTER 5

Training and the Depot

BRITTON (joined 1918).
The Depot was fairly rough. They kept you going all the time. You done an hour of physical training every day. You done three hours on the square with your carbine, it was a carbine that was the rifle at the time, the Enfield carbine, and school. You done two hours of school. We learned law. You didn't go out much, you know, from the Depot. In the Depot when you went in there first, roll call was six in the evening and eight and ten for the first two months, so you couldn't go away far then. At the end of the two months you attended roll call at six and ten to keep you from going out. Well once you got your uniform, that was a month or six weeks probably, you daren't go out in civvies, you had to go out in uniform that was the rule. And another thing, you see, you had to have a cane, you wouldn't get past the sergeant and the guard without the cane. I suppose it was dress. It was part of the work. In the winter time you always had the black gloves and you had to wear them. If you were caught out [without them] you were for it. It was very strict. If you wanted to go out you had to grovel in front of the Adjutant and get a pass, get permission from him to go out in civvies. The only day you got out in civvies was the day before you left to go to the country, to go to your station.

Well, you had to have an ordinary education, and they put you under a strict medical. You'd do three hours every day, three hours school every day and two hours drilling on the square, and an hour of gym and physical exercise. If you made a mistake you'd be probably kept on another month. The first month you drilled without arms but then you had the carbine and you were drilled with the rifle all the time. I enjoyed drilling. They had what they call a Head Constable Major; he was in charge of all the drilling, and there was so many drill instructors. Well then one squad went out and other recruits came in. But this one Head Constable Major he was very, very strict, you know, but he wouldn't hear of any recruit being abused or anything on the square. Some of the drill instructors would've liked to abuse you if you

44

didn't do it right. It was a semi-military force. It was just like drilling for the army, I'm sure, although I don't suppose the army did much schooling. We did more schools. Well then, you had to fire your rounds the same as a soldier. You were taught with the revolver as well.

BROOKES (joined 1920).
I went down to Mountpottinger [in Belfast] and sat my exam, then I went to the Commissioner's office and sat another exam, and I passed that. Then I went to Phoenix Park. We did a bit of dictation and first rules in arithmetic, multiplication and subtraction. I was able to do that alright. You got some [recruits] that lived in big towns and all, had a better chance of education than we had. We had to walk two miles to school and two back. Sometimes you were wringing wet, the water running out of you before you got there. It was very unpleasant sitting there; and there were days we never went near school at all. You would get ones here that lived in towns and they had a better chance, they had no distance to go to school and that's why you will get a difference in the police, with some better educated than others.

I never objected to training. I liked it alright. I got on fairly well in the training. The food wasn't the best. Sometimes they put the grub all out and if the sun was shining and it was warm it was sort of half toasted, but they went in a lot for corned meat and things like that. It wasn't too pleasant. I got on reasonably well at the schools. I remember one time the Head Constable called me out along with another man and he said, 'look, I want you to harass this fellow Colby'. Now he went and laid hands on him and touched the man, 'I arrest you for stealing a pair of shoes from such a place in Dublin and you need not say anything, but anything you do say will be taken down in writing and used in evidence against you'. So he said, 'you did that very well but I can't congratulate you on your manners'. He wanted me to call him 'sir', and you're not supposed to call anybody 'sir' only a District Inspector [or above]. They taught that the prevention of a crime was better than a detection – prevent it rather than detect it. You had what you call a Manual and it was simpler than the Police Guide. Well when you were passing out on that day you were just asked certain questions and if you were able to answer them you were through. I passed out alright. No contact with the locals. Only one person you could say was a friend.

CRAWFORD (joined 1920).
After I left school I went to Monaghan when my father purchased the farm there and I worked on my father's farm until I joined the RIC on 7 June 1920. The ordinary recruit was required to be between the ages of nineteen and twenty-seven, and be five feet nine in height and have

a thirty-six inch chest measurement. The policeman's son could join at eighteen years of age and at five feet eight in height, that was the difference. I liked the farm work, I liked the farm work alright. I was the first of the family to join. I went to the Depot in Dublin from the farm but I always wanted to join the police force, because it just came natural to me. I wanted to be in the police although I had no fault to find with the farm. I went to the Depot in Dublin for my six months of training. There were four companies there in the Depot; there was the Commandant, the Adjutant, the Head Constable Major, a Musketry Instructor and several Drill Instructors on the staff. I found it pretty hard at first until I got accustomed to it. At that time it was all military training, you were got up by the bugle in the morning at six o'clock, reveille went at six and tattoo went at ten at night, and you answered roll-call. From six in the morning till five in the evening you were continually at drill. At school we did Acts of Parliament and all sorts of police duties. The whole day was taken up and you never had more than about fifteen minutes between each, either school or drill or gym. We were taught bayonet fighting and the usual military stuff.

The food was very good, the food was good and the conditions were good. You had a bed made of straw, a palliasse filled with straw, what was known as a pillow, the same, a pack of straw for under your head and another bed. We just had to tie ourselves in or you rolled off. The country fellows that were used to a big wide bed would roll onto the floor. So you tied the sheets at the top of the bed, bring them right down and tied them across your feet and then you could roll round any road, you were tied in. The beds were hard, they were as hard as that floor but you got up fresh in the morning, glad to get out.

I liked Dublin but you weren't allowed to roam about through Dublin, you know, you were kept strictly under control in the Depot and you had to get a special pass to get out into the city; but I liked Dublin. We had what they called the wet canteen and the dry canteen in the Depot, so you could go in there and have a pint of beer at night and sit down and talk to all hours in the canteen. There was no need to go out. In the dry canteen you bought stuff, and you could go in and get a cup of coffee or something like that. In the wet canteen you could get pints of Guinness's stout, thought you were floating up the Liffy.

I didn't find the schools easy. There was a District Inspector supervised the schools and there were Head Constables in charge of teaching the schools, and you were issued with the Police Manual. I think the one I had was 1909 Manual, it gave a synopsis of various Acts of Parliament in litany form, question and answer and so forth. That's the way, and it was quite easy to pick up. You had to pass out, of course, at the end of it. The odd one didn't pass out. As a rule they walked round to Marlborough Barracks [now McKee Barracks] and joined the army, just at the back of the Depot.

In the Curragh [where some recruits were moved following a big recruitment drive among ex-servicemen] we went into wooden huts there to finish the training. Of course, it was a big military centre then, where you got sent for your training, big, big military centre, a lot of soldiers, army canteens and all that sort of thing. But it didn't make much difference to us, the regulations were the same, reveille went in the morning at the same hour, tattoo at night. There wasn't so many local people came into the Curragh, Newbridge was the nearest town there and the town of Kildare on the other side. We used to go in there an odd time, but they didn't allow us to roam around too much. I found it alright and most of the drill instructors were ex-Irish Guardsmen, police who had served in the Irish Guards during the war and were just back in 1918. It was Irish Guards drill at that time. At the end of the training we got three full weeks of musketry, nothing else only musketry, rifles, mills bombs, handgrenades and so forth.

CROSSETT (joined 1920).
I remember I was getting my ticket [to go to Dublin] from the conductor, you see, and he says, 'you're another bloody bugger going to the police', or something. He knew where I was going rightly and that time trouble was beginning to get rife. But I went to Dublin and then the Black and Tans began to come in, and Dublin Depot wasn't big enough and they needed more forces to cope. I finished my training in this Depot at Swords, on the way to Dublin. I had no complaints. I was a healthy, big fellow, I could ate anything. I didn't complain.

I've sad memories. I wasn't able to read well and every school was a battle and glad to get it over, you know. I picked it up, I had a great memory. I knew the Manual and the police duties and the answers to all the things, a great memory, but at the same time, like, I wasn't a good policeman. I was a good enough policeman, I done the work as well as any of them, but if I had been left on my own, like, I would have been hopeless. The drill was lovely, great. Phoenix Park had a great parade ground and Spud Murphy was the head drill master, he was a terror. He would a jumped a foot off the ground every command, and it was powerful to hear the Peeler and the Goat, the tune, you know, and the brass band, we had a great brass band. I was good at drill. I was a great shot too. You used to set your rifle on the tripod, and you had to take an aim for the bull's eye and then screw the tripod in so that the gun couldn't move. I seemed to be good at it. I was a great shot when I was a cub [scout]. When I was thirteen I won my first competition in rifle shooting. I was the best shot in Dublin and I used to be able to shoot partridge creeping up the stooks over on the other side of the road when you'd be walking along the road. I could have shot a partridge with a revolver, a Webley revolver, and I shot rabbits with the rifle.

I didn't know what to think [of Dublin], couldn't compare it with anything. You didn't get out much through Dublin, the trouble was going on then, you could have been shot. Dublin people were, anybody I met right down through Ireland, were all very nice people.

DUNNE (joined 1917).
Well, the food was rough but there was plenty of it, you were well fed alright. The bedding was rough too, you know, at that time it was straw beds, you know, the pillows were filled with straw and even the mattresses, everything had straw. But of course, being young and hardy, I suppose, it didn't affect me, I soon became used to it. Well, of course, I was very active at the time and I was very healthy; I was a bit of an athlete in my time. In the Depot I jumped six feet, of course that's only a small jump now, but then it was a big jump. In fact I remember being in the gymnasium and the instructor wanted to know if there were any jumpers in the crowd and a fellow put up his hand, I remember. Strange later on, I was home on leave in Galway when I was on the RUC and who did I meet but him serving in the Civic Guards. He resigned before me, you know, at the time of the trouble and he joined the Guards. I liked the drill but it was very severe, they were very severe, you know. I remember running across some of them, there was a bit of a devil about me and they wouldn't take that. I remember another chap and I were caught several times codding and going on, you see, in the gymnasium, and we'd get the rope, up and down the rope four or five times, and we were told to go over and stand at the sergeant's desk. Later on we were caught doing some mischief again and it was out on the square, that's where they drill, you see, and there was a white line right round the square and he doubled us round there for about ten times. Then he brought us in and he gave us the works, and I saw this fellow, he was a Mayo man, I saw him crying with temper and he wouldn't give in, you know. I liked the schools. Things were very tight, they were very severe, you know, it was a very hard six months. When you left there, I'm telling you, you were well hardened, you were. I didn't care for the city, you know, and, of course, while we were there in the Depot we hadn't much time. We were kept at it, you weren't allowed to go out except maybe for a couple of hours in the evening.

Well, of course, you had to go through an examination. I think there was three examinations in all coming up, and then the final. The Commandant had you out there in the square and then you were taken in the school and you had to pass through all those things. We worked fairly hard, you know, I mean you had to, you didn't want to be put back. There was only one person put back. Now at that time when you were going to your stations you didn't get your own county or the adjoining county and strange there was only one man going to Kerry, he was a chum of mine too, he was going to Kerry. I suppose they wanted extra men out in the country and I was sent to Kerry, and another chap was sent to Clare. He was shot afterwards in Clare. There was a big number of them shot, you know, later on in the 1920s, a big lot of RIC shot.

GALLAGHER (joined 1918).
Phoenix Park was tough, it was far worse than the army, the drill, oh, it was tough, although you were glad to have some kind of a job. You didn't have the time or money to see much of Dublin. We had a few army recruits when I was in the Depot. The drill made you physically fit, do you see, built you up, straightened you and made you put out your chest a bit and all that. School was alright. It was all learning scraps of Acts of Parliament here and there. Food was plain and a bit rough. It was a bit stale; there was hardly any of the recruits that put on weight.

GILMER (joined 1919).
I went to the Depot and there was another chap with me from my part, he was an ex-serviceman. We had to go to Cavan on the sixteenth and then to Dublin after. We were examined by a doctor in Cavan and we were examined by a doctor in Dublin too. When I arrived in the Depot I got a threatening letter from the IRA but I ignored it. It was sent to me in Dublin, and there was another young chap in the Depot from my part, and he got a threatening letter too. His father and his brothers, they were cattle dealers, and they did it on a large scale too; he went to America after. He came to see me since and he was in a bad way for what he'd done. He wished he had stayed in the police. Ah, they [Republicans] didn't do anything although they threatened to kill me. When I finished in the Depot and got out to my station I got four days holiday to go to see my parents. There were a neighbour man came over to me, he was a farmer, and I used to do his ploughing. He told me to get away and that they were coming for me tonight. I laughed at the idea of it and he demanded and all, he was serious, you know, he wouldn't like to see anything happen to me. He wasn't one of the fellows that would go for trouble and he persuaded and persuaded and in the end I went down to my uncle, who drove me to the railway station. They went to my house and they went to my uncle too, looking for me, yes. They meant work that time.

There's one thing I must say about the Depot, the discipline was good and the food wasn't bad at all, it was alright. But they [fellow recruits] were nice. I remember there was a big parade. Sir Nevil Macready was there, General Macready, and we were allowed off. Myself and a chap called Boffin went to get our photographs taken down the city and we put a civvy coat over our uniform, but we were fired on.

Dublin was alright. We mixed with just ourselves. Really at that time when I was a senior recruit I had to go to the South of Ireland on escort with steel shutters [on the vehicle], and when you went into a shop in the South of Ireland at that time for anything, you had to lift it and pay for it just, they wouldn't serve you. They wouldn't serve you at all. I was in Roscommon and then I was down in Cork, and even at that time they were blowing up bridges a lot and we had planks to put across. After the Depot I got Derry city where the riots were on, but in the Depot, as a senior recruit, I got a lot of escort duty.

Military drill was stiff. Do you know, it was Irish Guardsmen that were instructors, but I enjoyed it; when you get used to it. At the first it was a wee bit rough. But they were very nice in the Depot too, and the officers. There was a guard on the officers' quarters and one night I was on with another man. He thought the IRA was coming but it was a deer in the bush. But he fired a shot anyway, and he had to explain about it. Oh, the schools were pretty stiff but I liked them well.

McIvor (joined 1920).
It was November 1920 when I joined and five of us went to the Depot from County Antrim, and of course we thought they would provide a bed for us. But when we went there we were given a palliasse and told to fill it with straw. Oh the conditions were rough, very rough, and of course most of them stuffed it [straw] in, and it was too round and when they lay down on it they fell out the whole night between the beds. The mess, oh it was terrible. You'd smell the cheese from about a hundred yards, if anybody got cheese out you could smell it. The first morning that I was there getting the breakfast, there was black puddin on the plate and they were enamel plates with pieces broken out of them, you know, and they were black, they were awful looking. I had never seen black puddin, it was never in our house, and I asked the fellow next to me, 'what's this?'. 'Not like it Mac?', he said, and he just snapped it off my plate. But the mess was terrible. They'd have an Orderly Officer come in every now and then and ask for complaints. This fellow sitting beside me, an ex-soldier, jumped up and said there was a tape worm in his bacon. 'Well, what's wrong with that', and he replied, 'well sir, would you eat the bugger?'

The Depot from morning to night was drill, physical training. There was an occasional open day where the band played on the square, and old members trooped in, but not very many of them. In the Depot there was the transport yard and we had to walk up and down it you see, on sentry duty. There was no such thing as rubber heels, shods on your boots, as they used to say on the square, 'I want to see the sparks flying when you're marching'. The railway ran below the Depot yard and the IRA could hear us walking, so they decided it would be a good thing for to put a bit of ammunition in and blow us up. But one of them, whatever sort of a tool he had, it hit the line and the army heard it at the far end, and they opened up. They didn't try that again.

Ach, it was a hectic time. What I remember most is the lack of nourishment; when you'd come back the mess was closed, next morning parade at 4 am to go to bring in recruits coming from England, you got no breakfast. You waited to get your dinner and it wasn't worth anything, it was terrible. And the jam, it was surplus from the First World War and you had to cut it with a knife. It was just the taste of turnips; it was like chewing gum. Oh the recruits' mess it was terrible.

There was one Viceroy, a lot of police were parading to receive their Constabulary Medal. They were lined up at the Depot. Now when a man is asked to present a medal he's in his full uniform; he [the Viceroy] came in an old smoking jacket and slippers. I considered it as an insult.

McMenamin (joined 1920).
The first shock I got was as I sat down to the table for my dinner and I reached for the spud the same as I did at home. When I'd peeled the one, there was no more, they were all gone. The boys that were used to it put them down their trousers to conceal them; they'd pinch the food. You were very badly fed at that time. You got two slices of bread in the morning, no eggs, nor no nothing, you got the egg of a Sunday morning and a spoonful of porridge on a plate with the egg sitting in it. I didn't stay there long before we went down to the Curragh in County Kildare. I had plenty of moving about but it was no time till you got in with chaps, fine fellows, oh the best.

The RIC was pretty militarized. It was always an armed force you see. They'd bombs and everything else, they had bombs and machine guns, the whole lot, and Rolls Royce armoured cars. You were taught to know how to use all those bombs, machine guns and everything. Well we had special training for the machine guns, they all didn't go for that.

Sterrett (joined 1921).
I was in Donegal, you had to leave at 5 o'clock in the morning, four of us, because times were very bad. A lot of them didn't like the police

see, and we had to be careful, had to leave at 5 o'clock in the morning. I had to be in Letterkenny, that's Headquarters, at 9 o'clock to pass the exam, and then we'd to pass the doctor. When we went on to Dublin we had to pass the doctor again. I went in with the sergeant and I passed the exam, he put you through a preliminary exam, and then you had to go and get your birth certificate. So we had to go away up in the bus about twelve mile for to get the birth certificate you know. The other chap was a cousin. You had to sit an exam and it was generally a soft thing, you had four addition, four subtraction, four division and four multiplication see; no three of each, that was twelve sums. I was good at the figures and there was a man going up and down, he says to me 'can you not do them?' Says I, 'I've them all done'. So he lifted them to see if they were alright. They were all very simple. I remember then he gave us dictation out of the Code. There was words in the Code that the ordinary person wasn't used to. I remember I had three misspells, three, and others had more, but he allowed you two. But he says, 'I blame myself for that', he says, 'I blame myself so I won't count that'. Anyway we passed. Well then we'd to pass the doctor. Height, chest measurement see.

I remember at Christmas time we got word to be in Letterkenny at 9 am on January 14th see, so that was the two of us. There was four of us went altogether. On the way to Dublin, when we were at Drogheda, a wee lad run past and he threw something in the window and one of the boys lifted it and looked at it. He opened it, 'don't be throwing your eyes about you, you'll sell yourselves'. So anyway that put the wind up us. So when we arrived in Dublin, we were only raw, and we heard about the IRA men being in policemen's uniform. There was one man come over to us he says, 'are you the five' – there was now another one – 'are you the five recruits from Donegal?' I says we are. 'Will you follow me.' There was a sergeant and nine men there, 'sergeant here's your five men here'. So he took us out and we were about to get into a big tender and he says, 'now keep your head low because there was shooting on the way down'. He thought that was a joke! So we landed up in Dublin where you started training.

I had a cousin living in Dublin and we used to go down in civvies. The other brother, he was working in Belfast, and he come to see me on Sunday when I was in the Depot, and when he came to the gate they wouldn't let him in. Says he, 'I've a brother here', says they, 'anybody could tell us that'. We were away at church service and he was outside the gate, and we were marching in carrying the rifles. We were marching in and I waved to him. Oh you had to be careful. You had to go out in civvies, they wouldn't allow you to go out in uniform.

Oh the food was alright, very good. I thought it was alright, but I'd never that big an appetite you know, but I found it alright. We were very raw at first you know. We had a sergeant instructor there and he was from the Irish Guards, man he had all the old army slang. He'd say 'don't think you're hanging to your mothers apron strings now'. He says 'you're on the army now'. Man he was tough, oh he was tough. There was another man there, he was great you know, we thought he was a good instructor.

In school we did Police Regulations and Acts of Parliament. There were regulations regarding food; if there was only one sergeant in the mess he must dine by himself see, and you had to go in properly dressed. So this sergeant checked me for coming in for my breakfast, I hadn't my frock. Well says I, 'sergeant if you're going to live by the regulations you'll have to comply with them', Says I, 'sergeant, the regulations state if there's more than one sergeant they must dine by themself'. Says I 'sergeant if you're going to enforce the regulations I can enforce them too'. He drew his horns in, he knew he'd been well taken back. If there was more than one sergeant they must dine by themselves. They couldn't eat along with the men, they had their own cook and provided their own stuff. There was a messman, what you called a messman, he was appointed for a month, he supplied the stuff.

Recruits

CRAWFORD (joined 1920).
They were nearly all farmers' sons, countrymen from Cork and Kerry and Donegal, all over Ireland, all over Ireland. There were not many Englishmen at that stage but later on when the troubles increased, they recruited what was known as the Black and Tan crowd. Well, they were all Englishmen, English and Scotch. There were a lot of them ex-service men, ex-soldiers and ex-sailors, they were a mixed gathering.

DUNNE (joined 1917).
We did have a few officers when the English come, but recruits were all Irishmen and, of course, the majority of them were farmers' sons. There were two or three Cadets there at a time and one or two Englishmen, I remember. You couldn't mix with Cadets.

FLIGHT (joined 1920).
I went to Phoenix Park for training and I was there from March until September. I was allocated to County Clare, just about one of the hottest spots in Ireland. Recruits were nearly all Irish. They recruited some at that time, known as Black and Tans. They mostly were sent to Gormanston Training Depot, that's just outside of Dublin there.

There was as many Roman Catholics as Protestants, and all fine fellows they were, just as loyal as the Protestants.

GALLAGHER (joined 1918).
There was very few army men in 1918 when I joined, the war wasn't over; I joined in the spring of 1918. Most were Catholic of course; sure, the most of Ireland at that time it was nearly all Catholic. I didn't find any bother joining the police. The trouble hadn't started. Where I come from, the North, they would not mind you joining, but there was a lot of young fellows from the South was on the RIC. They wouldn't be welcome at home once the trouble joined.

GILMER (joined 1919).
Recruits were mostly all small farmers' sons. The ex-servicemen got no training at all. The ex-servicemen got three or four days and then they were sent out. A good number of the farmers' sons were Catholic. Three-fourths of them were Roman Catholic. I suppose there would have been a couple of Protestants in my company, that's all.

McIVOR (joined 1920).
The only ones they were getting were probably from the North, and any that were joining from the South were policemen's sons.

McMENAMIN (joined 1920).
Ah, mostly farmers' sons, and failed bank clerks and schoolmasters who didn't reach the grade; plenty of qualified schoolmasters in it, a big lot of them well educated. The Catholic crowd that joined the police were ex-schoolmasters that maybe taught a year or two and left it and went to the police. Most of them studied there, they studied a lot, a big lot of them promoted from the ranks right up.

STERRETT (joined 1921).
Aye well, five of us joined that morning and we were all Protestants. It wasn't that easy; there was plenty of chaps turned down, plenty turned down. They kept up their standards. When I joined there was five of us and we were all Protestants, but then when you went to a station two-thirds of them were Catholics. How you knew was on the parade on Sunday when you'd see the size of their parade and the size of ours.

SULLIVAN (joined 1920).
All our instructors were ex-army men, that was 1920, and some of them were just released from army service. There was a big lot of army men, more then ever I thought would have been possible. They were

very tough. At least we counted them tough because we were fresh meat from the country. They [the recruits] were nearly all ex-servicemem and sons of ex-servicemen. The man that I joined with he belonged to Galway West. He was a member of the Royal Navy and you daren't open your mouth and say anything about the navy or the army in his presence. He wouldn't stand any nonsense.

CHAPTER 6

Ordinary features of station life and work.

Officers and patterns of authority

BRITTON
There was a sergeant, he was transferred from Cork and who was under threat of death or something from the IRA. Well he was very strict, you couldn't please him, you know, and the relations weren't very good. It all depends, in a small station, on the sergeant; he's the boss. Sergeants used to note the time you went out, the time you came in.

BROOKES
Our officer was a very good man, he was from Clady. I done Orderly Duty for him. He says, 'you're alright as long as you're with me unless you commit murder'. Some of them could be strict, but generally I found that I never had any trouble with officers, I never gave them any cause for any trouble. I couldn't say anything bad about any officer that I served under. During inspections they went along, saw a man maybe with a crooked cap. 'Fix that cap on you', they'd say, or something like that. I had no trouble with any inspections. They'd send word, you're all prepared and all dickied up for it. You had to look after your regulation box, all your equipment and that.

CRAWFORD
Well, you had two classes of officers; you had what they used to call the Gentleman Officer, that was the man who went in as a Cadet, and you had the Ranker. Well, sometimes I preferred serving with the man who went in as a Cadet because the Ranker sometimes, he knew every rope on the ship and you could not pull wool over his eyes, which sometimes happened with what they called the Gentleman Officer. Some of them were strict. The sergeant was the main man in the constabulary, he was the pivot man. Officers were alright but the

sergeants, most of them were strict, and had to be. Some of the Head Constables were too, but any man that conducted himself as he should do, he had nothing to fear from any of them. You had inspections every month by your District Inspector and every three months by your County Inspector, and occasionally by the Inspector General. They filled in what they called the Inspection Book and there were various items in that that had to be answered, good, fair, so forth, clean, regular and all this sort of thing, police duties well known or not known, and anything that they discovered wrong. They wrote it in the Inspection Book and a copy of that went up to the Inspector General, and he judged the sergeant in charge of that station on these reports. Then there had to be night inspections, the DI had to carry out night inspections for any station that was within eight miles of his headquarters. Latterly you were told that your Barrack was expected to be in perfect order, clean and everything, beds made up and floors scrubbed and tables scrubbed and so forth.

You could use the opportunity to raise complaints. We'd make a complaint and they were told then to commit it to writing and it would be investigated. There wasn't so many complaints. From time to time pay would crop up. When I joined the RIC the pay was three pounds ten a week which was more than a tradesman had at that time, and was considered a very reasonable pay. Well, you paid for your food out of that and Barrack rents, you paid so much for the house that you were living in, your Barrack, you paid for that out of your pay too, so much deducted. You got a boot allowance of five shillings a week, that was for the boots that you wore on beat. You got a cycle allowance, and a married man got a rent allowance of one pound one shilling and eight pence a month. It wouldn't go far now in paying rent.

CROSSETT
We held nothing against them, nobody disliked them. I got on wonderfully well. One day I was out on parade, you know, you went out on parade in the morning to the yard. I had dusted myself and one policeman looked the other one over to see if you had dust. 'Oh look at that tunic of yours', he says, 'away and get the Barrack Orderly to brush you down'. Says he, 'I see nothing wrong with it'. I just went out again the way I went in, no brushes or no nothing. He looked at me and says he, 'that's better'. Ach now, there were some of them more strict than others but there was nothing wrong with any of them that I could see. There were no great snobbery nor anything at all, nowhere that I could see, but then again I wasn't a smart Alec.

DUNNE
I served with some very decent men and some of them, in fact, shouldn't have been officers at all by the way they could treat men; I

mean abuse, the abuse they give men, threatening to get them dismissed if they didn't have prosecutions. I knew an officer who was setting out to make progress and he upset the men. 'How many cases had you at court?', he would ask you. I mean, there was no serious crime, a case would be maybe, well, no lights on bicycles, you know, that would be the main prosecution that the police was having at that time. It was very difficult to get prosecutions. I remember one occasion in one of the stations I was in, the DI came on inspection and he wanted to know if you had any complaints. I says, 'I have a complaint for you'. Well actually to God, he jumped, 'what's your complaint?' But he stopped the problem. But the youngsters, the English Cadets, was very severe, you know.

Well, now, of course, the pay was small in the RIC at the time, and a letter appeared in the local paper condemning the authorities for the way they were treating the police with small pay. It was like 1920. The County Inspector went out to inspect a station and he must have suspected this acting sergeant for writing those letters. He mentioned the letters appearing in the paper, and he said that he'd like if the man would come forward and tell his grievance. He jumps up and says, 'I'm your man'. In a couple of days he was transferred, and later he resigned. At that time they were forming a police force in England, I think it was in Manchester it was. Knowing this he joined them over there. There was a circular issued then, anybody that had joined the Police Trade Union would be dismissed, but they were frightened of it being a strike. There was going to be a strike and I remember, of course, at that time we had no telephone. The wire came this Saturday night to hold on and the rise of pay had come, in fact our pay was trebled, I got something over fifty pounds, and I thought I'd never be a poor man again. There was certainly a fierce lot of people frightened [about a strike] but some policemen wouldn't join, especially aged men, a lot of the young men did join.

FLIGHT
They were strict, they liked to see the thing done properly, they were fairly sharp. There was no warning before hand about inspections, they just hopped in on you. They were fairly strict. There was no recreation for officers or constables, you were thinking of your work the whole time.

GALLAGHER
There was one night we had a DI, he was an ex-army man, what they called a Cadet. Well, he was an innocent kind of a boy. He'd go out and do patrols, and he would go out the road and he'd be trying to leap the ditches and everything; he was the only man bothered with that.

He was, sure he was, innocent or he wouldn't be leaping the ditches, making out there'd be an ambush here and there. The patrol that he'd be with had to practice leaping over ditches as if there was an ambush. He happened to be in Sligo town and he come home mortally wounded. There was a wee church, it was a real Catholic community and he used to go to it. After he got wounded, we sent for a Protestant minister to come and tend to him, but the next time we were told to go for the parish priest. I remember on one occasion two of us with the Crossley [lorry] were told to go for a priest. We had another DI, he was a Resident Magistrate's son and an ex-army man. He come to us the time of the trouble, and he done damn all. He done nothing at all, no duty, and he got away with it. He was down the town the whole day and first he used to dine with us, and sleep with us, but he went down the town and met some government men and he got in with them. He put in the whole day with them. He was supposed to be here running a big office and he never entered the office at all. There was a Head [Constable] Fallon and he was what they called one of the P-men [passed the promotion exam from the ranks], he was a gentleman. He was well up, he done the DI's duty in the office and you often hear tell of a man signing another man's signature, well Head Fallon did. There was the half-sheet; that's what you called the things [reports] you needed to send away. There was was an inch on the left that you couldn't write on. There were certain forms the DI had to send to the County [headquarters] and he never wrote one of them, the Head wrote them and signed them. He done the whole DI's duty, I tell you, the DI never went to the office at all. He only came in and slept at night.

There was some officers real bad, some of them a terror. The bad ones were all duty, pull you up for damn all. And some were lazy. Some of them officers were upper class, some of them gentlemen and some of them bad. Same as any walk of life. You get some men awkward, contrary or useless.

McIvor
Some officers were wicked men. Whenever I landed in (....) there was a fellow sitting by a wee miserable looking fire. I sat down beside him and told him my name and that I was a recruit coming on transfer. There was a great big poker and I gave the fire a couple of pokes and he snaps it out of my hand. 'Don't do that', he says, 'wait till you see the trouble I'll get into.' With that, in bounced the Head, white moustache and his eyes blazing. 'What sort of conduct is this?', he says. 'Sorry Head but this young fellow here he didn't know, he poked the fire before I could take the poker off him.' Then he tackled me. 'Get your kit out till I inspect it.' I laid out all the kit and I had six bullets

more than I should a had; they were issued to me seeing as I was always on dangerous jobs. And he says, 'how do you account for this?' I said they were buckshee. 'What sort of gutter language is that?', he says. The other fellow says, 'that's a word that the army brought'. He [Head Constable] was a (....), his family all left him, nobody would live with him.

There wasn't the same discipline in the RUC; it wasn't just as wicked as the RIC. The RIC was very, very strict discipline. Well, a sense of humour takes you through a lot of trouble and the camaraderie amongst the members. We stuck to one another. There was one County Inspector, and if there was a disciplinary file and him on holidays, it had to be sent to him on his holidays. He was a tough nut. This County Inspector would give no notice of his inspection and he would maybe go to a station four or five miles away, and he would say, 'where is the road down to this next station?'. And of course he wouldn't go to that station at all because he thought they'd ring them up and tell them. He bounced in and maybe got this fellow who had gone over to the shop and this wasn't recorded in the book. Now that was a simple thing but he made a big thing out of it; if you're prepared it saves trouble, you brighten yourself up and clean the place up and your equipment and all. He would just bounce in and parade you in the yard, and he would hold schools there and he would pick some Act of Parliament that he knew inside out and throw questions at you for more than an hour. You had to learn them off by heart nearly. Another DI, he'd come in and he'd have an exercise book with questions and answers written down. If the answer wasn't exactly what he had written down, he said you didn't know it. Then there was the 'Hue and Cry', that was a list of wanted people and their descriptions, and he'd ask round and round and round. You got fined if you didn't know them. There was nothing wrong with the rest of them at all. Major (....) was a very nice man so he was; ex-military man you know, it was him that recommended me for that special station that I didn't like; gentlemanly type of people.

I'd an old Code, I used to read through it, how things were laid out, so much hay and all that sort of thing, terrible regulations about any man that had a horse. Of course, they were few and far between. There was one man who was Sir (....), he was a sergeant in Fermanagh, that was the title and he got a lot of [marriage] proposals, as a matter of fact, a good lot from England, I suppose on account of his title. His County Inspector would salute him when he'd come on parade.

McMENAMIN

Ah life, it wasn't too bad. The officers, of course, had special treatment everywhere – Depot and everywhere else. They had their own messing facilities and all that. Generally speaking they were fine fellows. They were nearly all ex-servicemen that I served with there, officers from the 1914-1918 war.

You had the big few alright, you know, upper class. Our top man when I came, he was one of the finest men, an Englishman, he was one of the finest men there. He wouldn't be looking for faults and then the next man I had, an Irishman, he'd a been looking to see if the pointsmen's gloves were white and shining. Some of them here were very tight. I remember a District Inspector, he was a very, very tight man, his father was a ranker. I remember him checking a fellow for having a button out of the top of his tunic, and then only coming from a baton charge. But some weren't too bad.

STERRETT
The Cadets were worse, oh aye. They hadn't came through the mill you see, they just walked into the job, they hadn't the same experience. Of course you might get an odd ranker, what we called a ranker, he rose from the ranks, who was tight but mostly speaking they were all very good. See, they knew what you'd come through.

When we were out on patrol, well this fellow, there was no Cadet vacancy for him at the time, and he joined as a constable till there was a vacancy for him; his father was a big knob too. He was on the first relief, he was on what we called the first relief, at a quarter to six in the morning, so the night guard wakened you. 'Get up', he says, 'for the first relief.' He says, 'I'm constable (....) to you', and this fellow was fairly rough. 'I don't give a damn what you are', says he, 'get up for the first relief.' This fellow was very rough you know, but afterwards, it wasn't very long afterwards till he was promoted to Cadet. His father was a big noise; they were big farmers and they knew big estates. I think his father had a title.

The first relief, they called it the first relief from a quarter to six to nine. If you were on that you got another one in the afternoon see, and the next day you done from a quarter to nine to a quarter to three, and then you were finished, every other day. Down where we were it was good farming country, big pieces of grass, cattle and everything, up to the eyes in grass, great cattle country, plenty of money.

SULLIVAN
Officers made themselves upper class whether we liked it or not. Once he [an officer] got a bit of authority under his feet he kept it there just. There was a difference but I wouldn't say it was a big difference. The man that was in charge of our station was a man named (....), and once he came inside the station you'd hear him barking and chewing and one thing another. Some of them could be very unpleasant and others

quite the reverse. As I say, once a man got a little bit of authority under his feet he made sure it was there. They didn't as a rule spread themselves around and make themselves sociable to the men.

Mundane aspects of station life and work

BRITTON

I never had been away [from Donegal], except round the local area, because at that time the bicycles were very hard to get and you had no money, you had no money to buy any. I had to buy a bicycle first in the RIC. The pay was very small at that time. The pay was £4.9s.6d a month, there was a war bonus at that time, it was during the war that I joined, you see, a war bonus of 10s.6d. It made you up to £5. Well out of that £5 you had to pay your mess and buy your boxes. Well everyone had to have a box which the officer inspects every month. Your box was there but you never troubled with it, you just left it there for the next time. You had your suit of clothes, boots, shaving kit, shirts and pants and whatever else you have. The District Inspector had a district and his duty was to inspect every Barrack in the district; there's about maybe six or seven Barracks. Well, then the County Inspector he came once every three months to inspect the station. They looked for dress, equipment and all, and they looked up the books. The only book you had was the Guard's Diary. When you went out on duty you wrote that constable so and so went out at 2 pm or at whatever time and was inspected by the station sergeant. You had another book for crime, or anything.

In Killyleagh we lived in the station. If you were married you had a house of your own. There was only one married [at Killyleagh] but the wife lived away, the rules was that time that he must have lodgings within half-a-mile of the Barracks. You just had to accept it. On patrol we eased off. You went out and you'd yarn with somebody and maybe had a lie down, sit down up the road. We used to go into a house and play cards, a wee shop. This man had a wee shop and we used to go in there and play cards sometimes. I tell you what happened to a policeman in the Springfield Road [Belfast]. He was on the beat, and he was a very, very fond of a drink now and then, so he looks round and slipped in and had a drink. But somebody outside come in and told him the Head and sergeant were outside. It was the corner of a street, and one door was in the front and the other at the side. So they kept this under observation for a while. Anyway [the publican] knocked the end off this barrel, got the policeman in and closed it up again. So, of course, he had a lot of boys about there, they slipped out and got a handcart and opened the yard door or the store door and took the barrel, put the barrel on the handcart and got this chap into some other friend's public house. The Head and the sergeant was still outside. Round the beat the man went, hands behind the back. 'Where were you?', they said. 'I was on the beat.' 'You were in this public house.' 'No I was not. I wasn't in that public house today. I don't need to go in to it.' So they questioned him a lot about this but he said that he was on the beat. So that was very good until they come at him the next day. They says, 'how did you get out of that public house?'. 'I wasn't in the public house.' He wouldn't tell, he wouldn't spill the beans.

They [the RIC] tended to be fairly strict on the drinking part of it, but then there was a lot of those small stations, you know, way out in the country – there were only one or two houses near the Barrack – they'd nothing else to do when they were off duty. They did a lot of fishing. You were bound to go to church. The rules and regulations was that you were bound to go to church once in the month at least. This was part of the rules and regulations. No matter what. It didn't matter what church. You could go to any church, but when I was in Killyleagh the other three were Roman Catholics. Well then the fourth Sunday, it was my turn to go to church, so one of them relieved me. But it happened down South there's a man there that was always in debt, so he hadn't gone to church during the month. So, the end of the month come and the Head called him in and he says, 'were you at church, this month? You'll have to go to church or I'll have to make a report of it'. So the rest of the boys got him fixed up to go to church on this particular Sunday. I didn't know any man in the RIC was divorced, nor anybody that was separated. That was taboo altogether. You had to be very careful in that respect.

BROOKES

I was an outdoor bird, I was away with the dog whenever I was free at all, away with the dog and after rabbits; brought some rabbits home and we cooked them. There was very little paperwork in the station. We never bothered with schools, only when the District Inspector came, he would get them all together and ask a few questions. He asked very little on police duties, just asked about any complaints and so on like that. Our DI was from a place called Clady. I was later on his batman or orderly in Dublin Castle, he was transferred to Ship Street Barracks. He was in the Castle, you see, and every DI had an orderly. I was to go down and get him a cup of tea in the morning.

CRAWFORD

I lived in the station in Navan. All single men lived in the station, and you had to be single until you had seven years' service, till you could

afford to get married. We had a woman came in and did the cooking
for us and a messman was appointed, one every month, a different
messman every month. He was responsible for seeing that the provisions were supplied to the cook to deal with. He would look after the
mess, the provisions, and she did the cooking. The messman collected
the money off each man, he made it out and the docket went up on
the dayroom wall saying what each man had to pay. You paid him and
he went around and paid the traders in the town. That's how the mess
was run then.

The sergeant lived in married quarters. In a good number of
stations a sergeant lived with a family, but a sergeant's family had to
leave Barracks when they became sixteen years of age, they weren't
allowed to remain in Barracks after sixteen. Probably they'd be afraid
of, particularly, I think, young girls of sixteen, they didn't want them
mixing with men in Barracks. I think that's probably the reason of it.
After that they had to provide lodgings. You were told that you were
the policeman and they weren't concerned with your wife or family.

You did two patrols in a day, two three-hour patrols. You paraded
in the morning at nine o'clock under arms, that was with the rifle, in
the Barrack yard. You were inspected by the Head Constable to see if
you were clean and regular, shaved and so forth. Then you went into
the dayroom and a school on police duties took place. You sat in
school for one hour and then the duty for the day was hanging up in
the dayroom. You went along there and read to see where your name
was, and you turned out accordingly for patrol, escort duty, or
whatever it was. You got instructions going out, your sergeant paraded
you going out to see that you had your equipment proper, and that
you were clean and regular. Then he gave you instructions as to what
you were to keep a look out for on different dates, different things.
Different areas, different things, you acted according to the instructions the sergeant gave you. You were paraded as you came in off
patrol to see that you were regular, as they called it. We looked for
various things, according to the locality, you see. There weren't so
many motor cars on the road so you wouldn't concern yourself much
with that. Cattle wandering on the road at that time was very common,
they'd break out of fields. You were supposed to caution the people
first and afterwards if they persisted in allowing their cattle to wander,
you had issue a summons against them; and there were other things.
You got complaints from people, something was stolen from them or
something like that, you had to look into that, and check that in the
town there was no disorderly conduct, that footpaths were kept clear,
and traders didn't obstruct the footpath with boxes. General police
work. There wasn't much IRA activity in Navan.

You talked to locals. It was fairly relaxed. There was not much IRA activity in Navan, nor in the County Meath generally all over, there wasn't much. You see, they were all big land owners in that county. It was a good county. You would go out there and get away up on the top of the hill. Great view off the top of it all over the whole of Ireland. Sometimes we had to patrol the Boyne water there, along the Boyne river for the fishing, the poachers used to come in there. It was a great salmon fishing area, and you would have to pay attention to that and go round. The Boyne river flows down through Navan to the town, it's joined by the Blackwater, a tributary, and it's a good salmon river. You'd have to send patrols down there frequently to see that they weren't being poached. No poteen. They were all decent farmers. They didn't want any trouble. Most of them were employed, you know, by these big land owners. They were employed looking after cattle and so forth and, of course, Navan, now, is a busy town, there's a big factory in it. It's improved. There wasn't so many poor, what you would call poor people in it, they all had some work. There wasn't much crime, not at all, no serious crime. The IRA didn't affect us very much.

You had to be always on the alert and watch, but we never had any serious trouble. Men were sent down from the North to Tipperary for six months, you know, to give them a turn there and sent back again. They relieved the men that were down there, just didn't want to have them there all the time. They took men from the North. But Tipperary was pretty bad. I know of police from Donegal sent down to Tipperary for six months to relieve other men. In Navan you were invited to places like dances and so forth, you were invited like anybody else. I attended a good few of them. They were chiefly from Protestant girls who knew young fellows on the police.

There were quite a lot of ex-servicemen in the RIC, Irish Guardsmen, nearly all Guardsmen. Ah, they were all fine lads, fine fellows. I liked them, got on well with them. There were some great characters amongst them. I remember being on escort duty away down the South and there was a Crossley [lorry] load of us. We came to Athlone, and we went into a Barrack there, the dayroom. We had an order about that time, you see, to unload the rifle. In Athlone there was a big fellow called Lawlor, he was from Wicklow and he was an ex-Irish Guardsman. The Head gave us the order to unload. I was down at the end, all the rest of them slipped the magazine out and Lawlor, his cartridges just flew all over the place. The Head went up to him, he says, 'were you never taught to unload, why don't you unload like the other men?' 'Listen Head', he says, 'I loaded and I unloaded where the bloody maggots were afraid to put their head over the ground.' The Head didn't pursue the question.

We had all these different kinds of drill; we did the same drill as the army got, the same as a soldier. It was much the same as the army, just. You used to have to roll your greatcoat and put it across like a bandolier. There was a cape rolled round your belt, a holdall, knife, fork, spoon, razor, wobbling brush and (.....). I found the paperwork wasn't too bad, you know. You had quite a lot of books to keep and a lot of paperwork, but it was part of your job and you had so many hours a day at it, and that was it. You did so many hours of outdoor duties depending upon your rank, and so many hours inside at the paperwork. There was no such thing as hours, your work went on to eleven and twelve o'clock at night. You'd go and work in the office till twelve o'clock, and you went in on Sunday and did all the work that maybe was lagging back. There was no such thing as hours.

People would still come to the station looking for advice or asking you to fill in forms. They came with complaints, they'd come and get you to fill forms for them. They were never sent away without getting attention.

CROSSETT
It was a big Barracks, you know, and there was only one door into it and a Barrack Orderly is the man that's in charge of this big Barracks. The door gets a knock, the Barrack Orderly is the only one that's allowed to open it, you see. You go and you see who it is. You write down all the ins and outs, the coming in and going out. That went on for twenty-four hours. You didn't do anything the next day. You were allowed off the next day.

DUNNE
In Kinlair [possibly means Kenmare] we did the beat, we did the beat regular in town. A nice sized town and we had a Head, four sergeants and ten men there. We did patrols, in fact we used to patrol out towards the old station that I was in first. I moved from there in 1918. In town we looked, more or less, for drunks and disorderly behaviour, things like that. Especially fair days, we saw a lot of drunks and disorderly behaviour. We got on fairly well, good folk, good friendly air. In Kerry you could hardly go into a house without a son on the police or if they hadn't they had a brother. Kerry supplied a big lot of the old RIC.

(RES) So how did the locals take to the killing of RIC men then?

That's what we could never get over, of course they didn't like it, but there were no reprisals. I remember an orphan boy whose parents got killed in an eviction, who was raised by the police. The boy couldn't read or write and when he grew up he used to wander from station to station being fed. His nickname was the Colonel and he used to pretend he was doing inspections, he used to get the policemen to write in his book that he had inspected the station.

STERRETT
The pay was very small then [1921] and we had to feed ourselves out of that; mess, of course wasn't very dear. I heard my brother [also in the RIC] saying it took him about three years saving to buy a suit. It took about two years saving to buy a bicycle as well. You got five shillings a month for upkeep of a bicycle, there was no other mode of conveyance then. If you had to go to the court together you had to hire what you called a jaunting car, a horse and side-car. If you'd a prisoner you took them on that. You'd to hire it, you'd to pay for it, and then you claimed for it see. Of course you always got it, but of course the fee wasn't very much at that time, but nevertheless it was a lot of money when you hadn't money.

Relations between Catholics and Protestants in the force

BRITTON (Protestant).
Oh we got on, aye, aye. There was I suppose about 80 per cent or maybe more Roman Catholics in the RIC. They liked to have one Protestant in every station. Well, the other three cons that I was with in Killyleagh were all quite good. I was the Protestant and they assisted me, you know, instructed me what to do and all. But there was no hostility, they were all good friends. Some of them joined the RUC.

BROOKES (Protestant).
There were more Catholics than Protestants. In [District] Headquarters there was forty-two and there was only two Protestants amongst them. They were all very good, I got on well with them all. No trouble. Religion made no difference. It didn't make any difference, they were all loyal, fight to the last. There was only man [Catholic policeman] that we suspected. Only one man, who was the station sergeant, he could go anywhere without being attacked. The reason we suspected him was he went out one morning early and he come into the Barrack, and all the names was written down on a slip for a patrol [that was attacked] and he scored his own name out and put the other sergeant's name at the top. We suspected after that, that he knew the attack was coming off. You couldn't do very much about it because you would need to have more evidence.

CRAWFORD (Protestant).
There were about three or four Protestants in the station at that time. We had the very best of relations. Religion was never mentioned,

never was mentioned in the police in my time. There was no difference whatever made, none at all, never made any difference. You
could trust Catholics. I suppose you might get an odd one that would
think that way but I never came across them, I didn't know them.
There were Barrack Regulations hanging up in the dayroom, seventy-
two regulations, and one of them was that if a religious tract was
handed in to the Barrack Orderly at any station, he was to immediately
hand it to the man in charge who was to dispose of it as he thought fit.
He wasn't to leave in the dayroom or lying about or start arguing about
it, he was to hand it over to the man in charge of the station who was
to dispose of it. That was one of the regulations and there were
seventy-two of them. Some of them were very hard to keep, I can assure
you, and they weren't always kept. We did discuss politics, surely. Oh,
aye. Well we had various opinions about partition, you know. I think
the big majority of them would have preferred no partition at all.

CROSSETT (Protestant).
Aye, we thought there was a wee something about some Catholic
policemen. I thought (....), this fellow that was next to a man who was
killed, was just shady enough. I don't know why he picked himself a
front position. I suppose he thought that was maybe safer. We were all
were the same when I joined [1920]. Then the thing began to get
tighter, you know, and some of the boys, you'd a thought were backing
the Sinnfeinner. I mean, it was just like civilian life, some of them went
to church regular and some of them not so much. Politics wasn't
talked about, just some people were more pious or more religious
than others, it wasn't politics. The fact that you were a Protestant or
a Catholic wasn't important. It didn't seem to make any difference,
only coming to the last, I think maybe there might have been a bit,
beginning to get uneasy. Partition was never mentioned; I don't
remember talking about it. We weren't supposed to be politically
minded or have any differences in religion or anything else. You never
heard differences in people and it never annoyed me; none of the rest
of them seemed to bother, they were all having a right time of it and
they didn't care what you were.

DUNNE (Catholic).
Well they [Catholic policemen] didn't like partition, of course a lot
of the police then didn't take much interest in politics, at that time.
I didn't at any time. I never saw the slightest thing between them
[Catholics and Protestants in the force]. I never saw no difference,
you know. Regulations were very strict, you know, if anybody interfered with you or if you started a religious trouble, the authorities were
very sore on it, it was put down very quickly. But I never knew of any
trouble as regards religion.

FLIGHT (Protestant).
Relations were the very best. I mean to say, the Protestant didn't
interfere with the RC man's religion or anything like that, they all got
on together as one family, there was the best of relationships. Camaraderie was very good. You never thought of the like of religion, so you
didn't. It was like every other force, you nearly always suspected these
things to happen but I never seen, I never knew of any of it between
the men in the Barracks. Of course, there may have been something
like that going on and you actually never got to the bottom of it.

GALLAGHER (Catholic).
Oh, they [Catholic policemen] had nothing to do with partition. They
didn't give a hoot one way or another, as far as I know. A lot of men
that was in the RIC from the South of Ireland come North, I knew a
few of them about here that left to come North. They wouldn't be
welcome home, do you see, they had a wife and family, some of them,
so they come North, do you see.

GILMER (Protestant).
Relations were good. There's no doubt about it, the best comradeship
ever I witnessed was among the RIC. It was different when the RUC
and Specials got together.

MCIVOR (Protestant).
You see in Dublin Castle you had the enemy there, they knew
everything that was happening – infiltration by the IRA. DI Swazy was
transferred, he was an obnoxious person in Cork city and he was
transferred from that to Lisburn. They shot him coming out of the
church in Lisburn, shortly after he was transferred [he was shot on 22
August 1920]. They [Republicans] knew you see, got it all. I forget
how many officers came over and there was no accommodation for
them so they put them up in a hotel, and that night they shot the whole
lot of them, just went along the beds and just shot them. They
would've got it [information] there you see, in the Castle. We took
over the Castle from the DMP [Dublin Metropolitan Police], it was a
bit rough. They knew everything that was going on, it was very hard to
combat it. Among Catholic policemen there might have been a little
[support for Sinn Fein] near the end because they wouldn't show
their hand early on; I knew one fellow, I thought he was very bitter.

MCMAHON (Catholic).
Well, I was the same as them, I found them alright. I couldn't say
anything against them. Of course there was rows like, there used to be
plenty of bits of rows, you know, but it brushed over and passed. It was
not serious.

(RES) Some people have said that Catholic members of the Royal Irish Constabulary couldn't be trusted because they were in league with the Nationalists, what's your view of that?

Oh, gracious, I don't know why they'd say such a thing as that. It's nonsense. There was no such thing. They didn't. I don't see what they'd be doing the like of that, making false reports or anything like that. They did not, oh, no. I didn't think so and I didn't hear of anything, you'd jolly soon know if you did. I can't say there was ever anything like that.

McMENAMIN (Catholic).
There was quite a big lot of South of Ireland men, Kerry men, a big lot from what we call the 26 Counties now. A big lot of Protestants too. A big lot of the Protestants used to get stationed in Belfast, Portadown or the Loyalist parts. You never heard it mentioned, you know, you never heard religion mentioned in the Barrack itself. But if there was any vacancies and it was a Catholic place, they would have sent a Catholic sergeant there to deal with the people, you know, to get to know them more or less. Relations were good, the best of comradeship, really good comradeship in the police. But up here now [in the RUC], you see, when I come here first, there was supposed to be one third of every rank Catholic. As they died off, most of the Catholics were replaced by Protestants. In the RIC they were nearly all Irishmen. You'd get an odd one that come over here from England as constables and finished up as County Inspectors. The majority would have been Catholic. You never heard partition mentioned, no you never heard it mentioned. To tell you the truth I never bothered anything about any politics, no I didn't. There was no trouble at all, you never would hear religion mentioned. You had a religious parade every Sunday morning then, and every Sunday morning one sergeant marched the Prods, the other one the Catholics.

STERRETT (Protestant).
Oh no, no, religion never was mentioned, not at all. The Roman Catholics went to their church, the Church of Ireland went to their church and we went to our church see. Well then some of them was crafty, they said they were Covenanters or something like this, there was no church parade for them they hadn't to go at all you see. Relations amongst the men were good, absolutely. I tell you another thing, this fellow was a great smoker and he used to buy tobacco in a wee tin and he kept it in his locker. But he knew the locker had been opened and some of the tobacco had been pinched. He says, 'I'll stop that', and he took powder out of a cartridge and he mixed the two, not

too much see; he caught his man. Not too much and it wouldn't do much damage but man as soon as he lit the tobacco the pipe flew out helter skelter. He caught his man.

You'd never hear it mentioned. When I was there they were nearly all Roman Catholics, very few Protestants. They were clannish; the Roman Catholics would have backed one another see, but you had to live with them and it was up to you. Some of them were very nice. There was one Roman Catholic policeman when he got a drink taken, he would be telling them about the way the Protestants were shooting the Catholics in the North see, but that had got nothing to do with us. The other fellow, he says 'oh that's enough, don't be upsetting these fellows'. The Roman Catholic says, 'what's that got to do with them? Tell them to mind their own business'. Man this fellow got up, he was half tight you know, and he stiffened him, man dear, stiffened him across the bed. That was the end of it, there wasn't another word. He was a bitter boy. You met very few of them. Most were grand, grand, absolutely, wouldn't say a word.

SULLIVAN (Protestant).
Relations were very good. I never had any reason to think it otherwise, if the same thing existed today it would be a different world altogether. [As a Protestant] I didn't feel anyway out of place, quite on the contrary. There might be one or two, you know, that would be a bit slow in accepting you, maybe look at you dryly. There was never any feeling of disagreement. Some Catholics in the RIC liked it [partition] and others didn't. They never could agree on that; something like what it is now. But that feeling that there is now, well I don't know, that has arisen from all this drum beating and Orangeism and one thing and another, it leads to a lot of animosity between the groupings.

CHAPTER 7

Policing the troubles: the Southern experience

BROOKES (joined 1920).

I was stationed in County Waterford. They kept all the big, tall fellows for the city police, you see, and the rest went out round different stations. I went to a place called Ballyduff. It's just the same in Belfast there, at Castle Junction there, they used to have big fellas. It was just show. I got sent to Ballyduff, well I had a choice, I could have stayed in County Headquarters for I knew a sergeant. This was in (....) now, this was Headquarters and he said I was going to place called Ballyduff, he was the sergeant, he would get it changed and he could keep me in Headquarters. I said forget it. I went to Ballyduff and I never regretted it; they started to break it up in 1921. Sixteen people were in the station. I lived in the station, slept on a straw bed and a straw pillow. It was quite good.

We were ambushed once and in the Barrack we were attacked once, one fellow killed. There was trenches dug across the road and trees felled, and the sergeant went up to this house to make enquiries and they opened fire from a wee ridge on the patrol. They hit this fellow, that is one thing you're told, to take cover, first thing cover, take cover and shoot after. But he didn't get over the ditch and he was hit going over. He was just riddled with bullets. A few days after they ambushed the station. They had no chance of getting in there. It was an old military barracks or something. There were portholes to drop the bombs down. It was well defended.

I used to go out shooting duck and I had a dog, and that dog was never away from me. Ducks came in the evening to where there was water. But you had at least one patrol in a day, there was never any less than eight men went out on that patrol; a sergeant and eight men. There was two sergeants in the station. We were looking for nothing in particular, but you never knew where the enemy was. There was what you call Collins's crowd at that time, and he was on the move all the time and you never knew where he would turn up. They had no mercy upon anybody, Collins's crowd. We were basically looking for the IRA. No still of poteen, no light on your bicycle, no tail lamp, no anything, nobody bothered, the police didn't bother. It was just the police and the IRA. We had a cook, a woman, and they wouldn't let her cook anymore and we had to cook ourselves, you see, in turn. You'd do a month at a time, you know, that's what you call free mess. The IRA wouldn't allow them to cook. There was very few fairs near us, very little drunkeness. Patrols lasted three hours approximately, we were supposed to stay out three hours at a time.

The ones [members of the RIC] that were there longer than I were, they knew them better than I did, they knew all the suspects. I remember one day I went to church and I had two miles to walk and I went in, I was invited into a house and had my dinner in it and my tea. The sergeant he got alarmed, thought maybe I was kidnapped and he sent out a patrol, eight men looking for me. I didn't get told off for it but the sergeant said, 'glad to see you, glad they got you alright'. You never get any information from the locals [about Republicans], that's one thing you'd never get, they were afraid to tell anything.

CRAWFORD (joined 1920).
I was sent to the town of Navan in the County Meath. There were two stations in Navan; Navan number one and number two. There were thirty men in the one that I was in, it was number two. In number one there was a County Inspector, it was Headquarters for the county, and the District Inspector, a Head Constable and about twenty men. My station had a Head Constable, four sergeants and about twenty constables. It was a good, big station. Meath was a big, quiet county. I remember, I think it was the first time the race-course was open, there was a sergeant shot on it that day. But Navan was a good station and the people were very nice and friendly all round the town.

A lot of the Justices of the Peace, owing to intimidation or threats, resigned their commission and then the police would issue summonses against people for such cases as drunk or drunk and disorderly or so forth. These people wouldn't attend the local Sessions because the IRA were holding their own Petty Sessions at night in schoolhouses and places out round the country. They were summoning the men to them and our duty then was to go out and find out where these courts were being held, and to go out at night and disperse them and seize their books. We got the books by the sacks, I can tell you, seizing all round Petty Sessions, I don't know who appointed the Magistrates but they were acting as Magistrates, and they had their police. I remember doing beat duty in Navan after the Truce was signed on 21 July 1921 [the Truce was signed on 9 June 1921 and came into effect on 11 June], when the revolvers which we wore were taken off us. We were turned out with a belt and a baton and I'd be walking on one side of the street and IRA policemen walking the other side. He wore a soft hat and a trenchcoat and in most cases, I think, carried a revolver; he did his side of the police work and we did ours. But most of the people attended the IRA courts because they were afraid not to attend, and our job was to go out at night, though generally accompanied by a District Inspector, who'd go in and give them five minutes to disperse and seize their books. There was never any trouble. Among the books we got a lot of information about names and things. It was difficult sometimes to find out where they were holding them, it was generally in a schoolhouse they held them.

There wasn't much IRA activity in Navan. There was an ambush in Trim, that's eight or nine miles, in the same county. Not so much in Navan. Meath was a quiet county, very large farms in County Meath and they nearly all went for cattle rearing and that sort of thing. It never was what was termed a bad county for IRA work, no, it was not: Navan, they just never attacked it. Tipperary wasn't a great county to be sent to in those days, there was a lot of trouble in Tipperary and a lot of policemen shot in it.

CROSSETT (joined 1920).
I was sent to Bray, County Tipperary. The first shooting was in Tipperary outside the chapel.

(RES) Were you concerned about going into Tipperary?

No, I tell you, I was in an ambush. You were going maybe to Limerick gaol for somebody and then these boys they'd dug a hole in the ground on a bridge and you come along (......) and you had to pull up quick, you see, rather than go into it. Well, they were round the hills and would have shot down at you as soon as you showed up. I remember one day we were all going to the Petty Sessions, they burned the Petty Sessions office in (.....) where I was stationed, then we had to go to Cloughjordan which was a few miles away. This day there was ten of us, we had to cycle it too. We were ambushed in this corner, and I remember, (.....) was the first fellow, and at that time we were beginning to get suspicious of some of the RIC, maybe sort of stool pigeons, or working in hand with the Sinn Feiner. (.....) was the first and a fellow that had won a lot of medals in France was either with him or second to him on the bicycle, you went a space apart, two and two. (.....) from Scotland, Black and Tan, just had a bullet fair through the middle of the head and was killed. Well, there was some of the boys they wouldn't go home, you see, they wouldn't cycle home again, but three of us got on our bicycles and went home as if nothing had ever happened. That was the sort of fear that we had. I went to socials and dances, sometimes maybe it was dangerous, you know, but you went to church and to summer concerts. Relations were good, got out for tea an odd time, they were far kindlier than they are in the North. Work was hard and they were terrible nice people. I would go down anytime and live there. The boycott didn't have any effect where I was stationed.

We did school in the morning, but it was all on police duty and somebody that was wanted, and then a wee bit of arms drill. The old policemen knew very little about armaments. They had no armour. In the Barracks I was the only one that really knew much about a revolver or a rifle or anything else, how to load, and so on.

(RES) So then some of the older men who were not used to using arms had to be retrained?

They were surely. I remember (......) and the table was in the middle of the floor. I was sitting at the upper end of the table, and they were doing a bit of arms drill just round this big room. We had to learn to load and unload five cartridges – load, put it down into the magazine, push up the bolt, put your finger over the cartridge, push the bolt up over the cartridge, and then pull the trigger. Jeepers if this fellow, instead of putting the bullet down low enough, and damn it if the bullet didn't just pass me and stick in the wall behind me, chancey enough. Lots of fellows didn't know how to use arms. Some wasn't fit to handle a rifle and go out; they couldn't have protected you, protected themselves.

We'd patrol for three hours or more. There were some local stations closed, and we used to walk out there. It would take you a good while to patrol there. Devil the much else we done, I can't think of how we filled the day. We'd go gawkying down the road and look round and see if anything was suspicious or unusual, and interview somebody that could tell you something. It didn't serve much of a useful purpose as far as I could see, you just were there. We dealt with ordinary things if they came your way; that was still done. If a man was drunk, we used to chastise him and if he was very drunk we took him in. Oh aye, you done all the police duty but it wasn't very strict either. I never was involved in poteen. They got some poteen, after charging a man and all, then they dumped the poteen in the sink. Another fellow, he went outside the kitchen, you see, to where the water come out and he held a dish under it. He saved the whole. I believe round here [the area where he now lives] the police get no information from nobody; Protestants are afraid to tell it and the Roman Catholic if he doesn't belong to the Sinn Fein or the IRA, he's intimidated. In Tipperary we surely got a lot of information. We couldn't have done anything without it, we couldn't have lasted, but then it begun to get scarcer, but they were alright down there, there was nothing wrong with them.

A sergeant Blair, got his arm, a bullet. On a different time, we were going to Limerick for a prisoner, Well then, we come along this morning to the river, we crossed over on a bridge, there was a hole in the bridge, you see, we had to stop short, like, and then they started to shoot at us, but there were none of us hit. If you'd seen some of our policemen. They weren't great. They were great cowards, you know, some of them, feared of their lives. Started shooting (.....), didn't know what they were shooting at. The IRA weren't as good as now and they weren't accurate. I remember going away to Cloughjordan, I had somebody to see, I think it was a girl, maybe. I went on the bicycle, you know; a whole lot of them [police] wouldn't a went out, they were afraid. Jeepers when I was coming back, if there wasn't a crowd of the IRA or Sinn Feiners drilling in a field that I had to pass. I seen them, you see, and I just cycled on and went through and never was stopped or asked a question. I told them [the police] about it but there was no fuss, we let them drill away.

(RES) So relations with the local community in Tipperary were good enough for you to meet local girls then?

Oh aye, that's what I say. There was a girl who used to teach in the Convent, that was the Roman Catholic Cathedral, and she used to come out and see me quite normal. She was in the heart of the Roman Catholic church. We used to go and dance in Catholic houses up at the head of the town in the village, some of them were, like, nasty enough, and with a bit of jealousy would be sort of rough with it.

DUNNE (joined 1917).
I left the Depot after six months of training, and the first station was called Mulgrave along the Killarney lakes in Kerry. I was lifted to Killarney station by an old jarvey with a side-car and arrived at Mulgrave station at midnight. There were two other men there and our duty was for the protection of tourists and wild deer along the Killarney lakes, it was a very isolated place. My friend who had come with me to the Depot, another Galway man, he went to a station called Sneem in Kinnair district, and later I came to join him in Kinnair. One night he and a friend were kidnapped and neither of the two men were seen alive since.

We lived in the station. It was rough. It was along the Killarney lakes and our duty, more or less, was to protect wild deer that belonged to Lord Kinlair [possibly means Kenmare]. Of course, there'd be a lot of poaching there about, and then there were the tourists in the summer time. That was more or less our duty. The day was long, especially in this station because the nearest house was a little chapel about two miles away and we hadn't a shop in the district, there was one public house. It was a mountainous area and there was an allowance for an old fellow to visit twice a month in an old side-car from Killarney, which is ten miles from our station, and it was ten miles from Kinlair [possibly means Kenmare], so our station was called 'The Halfway to Travel': halfway between Kinlair [possibly means Kenmare] and Killarney. We had three constables, one was on the promotion list. You were all day guard for one day, you know, and didn't leave the station. Then next day you did two patrols, the next day you did two patrols, and the next day you were guard. On patrols you went along the road and had a chat with a farmer if you met a farmer. We carried no arms at that time. We used to go out at nightime and go along the road and, in fact, we'd go to a certain house and have a game of cards. There was a game-keeper there and if he was expecting anything he would send word to go over to him.

(RES) What did the protection of tourists amount to?

Well, to see that they weren't interfered with in any way. There was a place there called Queen's Cottage, a very nice little thatched cottage, the chairs were made of deer horns. It was a very nice place and a lot of people called, you know, tourists, especially English tourists. And you directed the traffic, of course, at that time there was very few motor cars, very few. You hardly ever saw the local Lord at all there, he was mostly in England. He had relations there. The Lords generally spent most of their time in England, they had summer residences there, you know.

I was in Kerry from 1917 up to 1922, just before disbandment. Well, of course, the times changed before I left Kerry, we were ambushed time and time again and our Barracks were attacked. I remember one occasion, one morning I saw a girl coming into the Barracks. We had a DI, a Head, two sergeants and ten men in the station. We saw this girl coming to the main gate and I called her over to say to her, and she says, I remember it was it was Good Friday morning, she was coming in to mass apparently. I knew the girl because I was at her father's house some time ago, there was some complaint, and she had a brother in the RIC who resigned and was shot afterwards. She says, 'there's a man lying dead out on road'. Says I, 'come on in'. She says, 'I daren't go in', and she rushed away. So the Head tells a couple of us to get our bicycles, follow her and bring her back. Fortunately, we met the sergeant coming in and he tells us to go back because it could be an ambush. We got the military and we went out with an advance party and we had to go through a cutting, the ground was high on both sides. Halfway through this cutting we saw them firing, and as we came round the corner and saw this man lying there, he was a fine, big lump of a man with the card round his neck, 'traitors and informers beware'. He had a bullet wound in the head. We examined him and he had very soft hands, you'd know he wasn't a workman. So the first conclusion we came to was that he was a policeman, you know, he was a big, tall man and he was like police material. So we took him up into the Barracks and got some people in there, nobody knew him. He was buried an unknown man. Three or four days later a woman comes. It was her son, an ex-army man who had been put out of the army during the war, he was a sort of a useless type of a fellow. He used to go round from Barrack to Barrack looking for an odd pair of old pants and any old boots. It was thought he was going in and giving information and he was kidnapped and shot. There was a tiny station called Rathmore some miles further on and the following month the same thing occurred. The Barrack servant's son went out for a walk and he saw this man lying dead on the road. The sergeant and six men went out to get this man and one man got back living, five of them were shot as they examined the body. They never expected there to be an ambush there and there was no protection.

In Kinlair [possibly means Kenmare] they decided on putting the military into the Barracks and putting the police out to the out stations. Well, we objected to this, to go out, and for two or three days we refused to go. Now at that time there wasn't even a telephone in our Barracks, it was a small out station and it hadn't even a telephone and up to the military arrived we had homing pigeons. If we wanted a message we had to release the birds. We released two birds with a message on their legs, and released them. But we had no information about other stations, but two other stations refused to go too.

(RES) Because of the danger?

Well, more or less, and they didn't think it was right that they should go out to the country stations and the military take over the Barracks. Now we had a very decent DI, and he let it go for two or three days and we decided then we'd go, but we didn't know that it was happening in the other stations. But in Listowel nine men walked out of the station and resigned. One went back to college, he belonged to Mayo and did some exams and entered the church. Our station was so isolated the police authorities wouldn't come near us, we were in a sort of a trap. If we were ambushed we would never get out of it. Things were getting bad at this time now and we decided that two men needed to do guard outside the Barracks at nightime. This went on for six months and finally we got the senior man to make a report, which was that if we weren't taken out of this station we would walk out of it. One evening a boat called 'Anthony Essex' arrived in Kinlair Bay [possibly means Kenmare] and took us on board, the whole business. Now we thought he was going to turn into Kinlair and land us in Kinlair [possibly means Kenmare]. The roads were blocked at this time, blown up and trenched, and bridges were blown up. But instead of turning into Kinlair he headed out to sea. A Scotsman took over the arms and locked them up. We arrived at Ennisfeirt, that's where Casement arrived in 1916, the famous Casement, and we took cover until the boat was tied up. When people saw this crowd of police they stopped work, so one of them says to us, 'you're not welcome here'. We went up to the Coastguard Station and phoned Tralee. In Tralee they didn't know what took us there. We left the boat, loaded our stuff and we headed for Tralee. The roads were blocked, the trees were cut down, we had to cut the trees to get through, but there was no ambush because they hadn't time, I suppose, to perfect it. So we headed to Tralee and we were there for two or three days when finally we were told to get ready in plain clothes, hand over our arms and told to take the train back to Kinlair [possibly means Kenmare]. I think there were five or six of us and we retraced our steps back to Kinlair [possibly means Kenmare] again. We came to the junction called Kettrick junction, where the military was ambushed one time. There was a man standing very uneasy, very interested in us, you see. Now we were in plain clothes and we had tea chests covered in canvas. So we went to question him to see who he was and he was the Head Constable going to our station on transfer, on promotion. He was coming from Larne, a very decent man. He thought we were after raiding some Barrack, that we were some sort of IRA men.

FLIGHT (joined 1920).
I was in County Clare, it was a great Barrack, they took over a hotel there and I think there were seventy constables, twenty-five sergeants, two Head Constables and a District Inspector. Big station. Plenty of room in it. It was a hot spot but I hardly ever thought of trouble from day to day. It wasn't as bad as it was in other parts. There was a place about six or eight miles from us and it was a fairly hot spot. We did patrols there maybe from fifteen to twenty miles. We patrolled in a diamond formation that was to prevent us being all caught out, and that went on from day to day. It would be up to six hours. There was a big school and lecture every morning. It was nearly all about defence of Barracks, protection on patrol duty and so forth.

Well, of course, at that time the traffic wasn't as heavy as what is on the roads now, it was very easy to deal with what traffic you met and stopped and searched. You'd be looking specially for the identity of the person, and there was plenty of poteen in that part of the country. It was very difficult to stamp that out. It was really the troubles that come first and you didn't bother so much about searching for poteen. I was involved in an ambush on one occasion. We had to travel from

(.....) for all our groceries and things like that, and coal and one thing and another. We were attacked once between Ennis Island and Ennis but there was no casualities, the attack was from fairly long distance from a field overlooking the road. I didn't come into contact with the IRA too much. I don't know that you could say it was peaceful but they didn't show up so much. I was quite grateful for that. Just a week before I left to go to the Depot in Dublin there was an ambush and there were six police knocked out that time, and that's the only roughness I saw while I was in County Clare. Nothing funny happened in my time. We didn't have much of a boycott, but dances was out of the question, there was no dances, it was too dangerous. Life was cut to a minimum.

GALLAGHER (joined 1918).
The South of Ireland was tough at that time. There was a couple of tough ambushes on the Auxiliaries. There was one ambush away down near Cork, they had four Crossleys [lorries] and the four was wiped out. Any that was saved was taken prisoner. Of course, it was their equipment they were looking for. I was based in the West of Ireland, in Sligo and Mayo. Oh, it was alright. We all went and patrolled; the roads and things. You wouldn't have much to do, there was no motor cars. You had to go out and do your areas, and if you seen anything or anyone that was breaking the law you were supposed to act, but there was very little crime at that time, till the troubles.

There was a Barrack that you lived in. There would there would be five or six with you at the most. The sergeants were alright, they were well up in duty, you know, they were well trained. You wouldn't be drinking too much. Pay was half-a-crown a day. It wasn't bad, it was average pay. We'd go on patrol carrying arms. We were all armed even in 1918. They were armed long before I joined. They were an armed force as long as I mind and for longer before that. They were an armed force for years and years. You wouldn't have a rifle till the trouble joined, you'd have a revolver, but you had a rifle belonging to you in the Barrack. If you were going on some kind of special duty you'd maybe have to bring a rifle with you. When I joined, one man patrolled in the daytime, two at night. And then patrolling when the trouble joined there'd be five or six on a patrol, even during the daytime. It was a powerful place for poteen making when I was up there in the West of Ireland. A powerful place altogether. Somebody from the station I was in, they caught them making it. They had information, of course, and they got the barrel of wash; it was a woman and her daughter living on a bit of land. I went out one day, no more than two hundred yards from the Barrack, and we met this young fellow coming with a pony and trap. He pulled up and chatted with myself, put down his hand in the trap and pulled out a bottle of poteen and gave it to me for to kill it [drink it]. When he took off the cork he told me to take a slug out. It was the worst poteen ever I seen. Well, I couldn't drink it. I found out after, he had the trap full of poteen, going to the next town to sell it and I wasn't a fortnight in the station, you know, it was a country place. How did he guess that I wouldn't bother my head? Patrolling was mostly to kill time; in a country area there was nothing doing. Not till the trouble joined it.

I was respected when I joined, but a while after I wasn't. When the troubles joined nobody wanted you, but before you were fairly well liked, fairly well. There was always a bit of a slur on them in places, surely, they belonged in the Establishment, you know, they called it that, the right word or not. But people were friendly until the troubles. Then you wouldn't have one to talk to you, they wouldn't talk to you in places. People in the West of Ireland particularly boycotted Belfast stuff; anything, drapery particularly, they put a boycott on it because it came from the North. They didn't want them even burning the coal. There was two boys in the drapery trade. Often we used to go in to kill time to chat to them, so they told us everything. They were in the drapery trade and they told us straight.

When the troubles got bad you could go out and you wouldn't know when you'd be fired on. I was fired on once, me and another man from Clare. There was two of us sitting in the dayroom after teatime and I was sitting with the heavy coat on, you know, the heavy coats, the police still have them. There was a three-cornered square in the town and a weighbridge in the centre of it, so we went in at the end of the square, and as we were travelling we met this man coming down to the Barrack. We bid him the time of night and no time left until we were fired on, and we run up the hill as quick as we could. Maloney says to me, 'I'll get them'. 'So will I', says I. I got it fair in the spine of the back, fair in the spine of the back, and the report was in the papers the next day, 'saved by a button'. The belt on the greatcoat, the heavy coats, you know, and on the back of them there a couple of buttons, you know, so it was there the bullet hit me. I wasn't saved by a button, that's what the papers said, but the bullet was defective, that's all the excuse for it. There was seven bullet holes in it [the coat] and only one of them hit me.

If you thought about being targets, sure you wouldn't be able to live. You tried to put that to the back of your mind. Sure there'd be nobody in the police if they thought of it that way. Of course, some resigned. I never thought of it. There was a lot of friends who tried to make people leave the police. Some of these Republicans would come round to a man if he had a son on the police and try to get him to resign, but this was more in the West of Ireland. There was an old man with us, Dermott, an old grey headed policeman who had long service. I didn't know him long but for years he never went on a holiday. So he said this time he was going on a holiday, and there wasn't a man in the Barrack but tried to prevent him going to Galway. He went to Galway and he never returned to us. They come at him. We were nearly sure that he wouldn't come back. They'd follow him and shoot him.

I tell you, in the shops, you'd go in, kill time and chat, they had no objection to us going in. Well, do you see, it was only when you didn't want to be very fair to everybody, and I was the junior man, it wouldn't be me who pulled the public up for breaking the law. It would always be a senior. The IRA, some of them were gentlemen, and you'd meet the odd twister. Just the same as the ordinary public. They'd ball you off, as they say, knock you down with the gun, but that was their job. In the West of Ireland, you'd meet very little Protestants, but we wouldn't be a bit better in with Protestants than Republicans. We'd be less better in with them. They'd have less to do with us than some of the Republicans, because they were afraid to be accused of giving us news, so they kept away from us altogether to keep safe. Ah, they were dangerous days, but sure you got used to it. I couldn't say you looked back on it with pride. Sure there's none of them proud of it. Are the Republicans proud of it? Are the British proud of it? There was nothing to be proud of. Sure when they look back on it, they know they were guilty of shooting and when they look back on it, sure they couldn't have pride in shooting a man.

McIvor (joined 1920).
I had the distinction of being the best recruit on parade and got a special station. I was paraded before the Commandant and he looked me up and down and turned round a few times and said it's unheard of, a recruit getting the County Dublin, because it's the choice county of Ireland. You'd think he was talking in the past nearly, because it was all in a bad state. I went up to the station that was in the Phoenix Park and it was the Vice Regal Lodge. The DMP [Dublin Metropolitan Police] had been there doing the gates and they shot the helmet off one of them. They were unarmed and they left, so the police [RIC] had to take it over, all the different gates right round it. Lord French was there, he was the Viceroy. All the duty up at the Vice Regal Lodge was done by rifle and bayonet, march up and down, it was an awful station. The Wiltshire Regiment were right round too, partly entrenched. I was coming one night off duty about two in the morning and there was a path, you daren't show a light, and being a stranger I wasn't too sure of the path, suddenly my cap went off and I drew the revolver but walked on. I was expecting a shot, so I went into the

Barracks and told them and he says, 'well, that has happened before, there's a branch, one's solid and the other comes up and down past like that and it has knocked the cap off a fellow before'. And when I went back my cap was lying there.

Then I come back on to the Reserve Force from the Vice Regal, that meant that you were rushed to every place that was in trouble. I was about six months in the Vice Regal, I think the station sergeant asked for me to come back again because he couldn't get men [to volunteer] and he says to me 'you never ran away'. He would be looking for men that were recruits to go on an escort, and when they saw him coming they'd all disappear to avoid going. I didn't do that. Well then while in the Reserve, there was a whole lot of queer things happened. Once when we were down in Cork we were going with spares [provisions] for different places. The roads were white in those days, and they [Republicans] could see the convoy coming for miles. We had big Leyland lorries with solid wheels on them. We went into the station to divide the load we had to take and a man says, 'they're watching you'. We got into the van and there was a shot rang out and I put my head out with the rifle; off went my cap. My pay was in it, my month's pay, lost the lot, just a trickle of blood because they were down below me. I was lucky enough.

Then when they opened the Parliament here in Northern Ireland, 1921 I think it was, King George attended, they brought a hundred of us up for to help to line the route. Of course it was the usual thing, best uniform and best everything. When we landed up we were put in horse show grounds on the Albertbridge Road, into the stalls where the horses were. They took the horses out and threw down some straw and put a blanket on it. That was for the good uniform, I tell you it wasn't going to be very good. After the parades we were to return, there was a wire from Dublin Castle for to catch this special train, the military were at each end and the horses in the middle. We missed it because some fellow pinched the other fellow's laces and they couldn't get one of his blankets. We had to march to the Great Northern and just as we went in, the train tooted and they wouldn't let us through. So we caught the next one. But the train we should have been on was bowled over, horses and all killed. We were lucky. The IRA lifted a section of the rail and the old train tumbled over and over. There was one station, the IRA surrounded it. There was about two hundred IRA surrounded it and they practically shot it all away, and when the ammunition was finished they [the RIC] come out and charged them. I wasn't in that but I went down to see it.

In the Reserve I'd be maybe in London at Scotland Yard today, and tomorrow I'd be away in Skibbereen. One particular time I came up from Cork and we landed in at four in the morning in the Depot in

Dublin and we were told there was a load of stuff urgently needed for Newtownards. It rained the whole way from Cork to Newtownards and we got nothing to eat, we were starved. There was one particular van went from the Depot to the [Dublin] Castle and it was hit every day. It had sides and they were very good too because it was like a light covering of steel and bagging in between and it only dinged it. Every time they'd came in they put a ring round the extra ones [bullet marks], three or four. Ach, you see they had to have despatches taken and one thing or another like that, so that particular van had to be out. And then in Limerick city they had to commandeer every bite they ate because they'd start up the Crossley [transport vehicle], we got a new fleet of Crossleys at that time, and they'd start it up, open the gate, shoot out down into the butchers, cut off a lump of beef and throw the money in the thing, and away.

Well, we looked upon all the whole lot of them as enemies because the Protestant people were with us all the time but the others were terrible. They used to dig trenches across the road you see, in the early part, and then camoflague it and of course down went the front wheels, and then they had an ambush. But we got wise to that, and used to carry planks for to cover this trench. Ah it was hectic. At the third day without getting to bed the Orderly Sergeant came and asks me out again. That was three nights I was out of bed. I sat all night at the north wall to protect a load of ammunition sitting on the quay, aye, about ten or twelve of us, sure we were complete targets.

Then there was a lot of men brought over from England you see, ex-soldiers and the Auxiliaries, well they were really hated. The Black and Tans were men who returned from the war and they hadn't uniforms for them. Oh the Black and Tans were in among us you see, they were just ordinary RIC, but they hadn't them fitted out with the proper uniform, coming back from the army. This war was the only one the RIC didn't take part in, they were in it from the Charge of the Light Brigade. But they weren't allowed this time to join any branch of the service, of course there was plenty of trouble at home.

We were well armed. But a very dangerous thing we did, and that was take the pin out and hold it in your fist to be ready to throw it. But if that man had been wounded and he'd open his hand he would have killed all round him. You see they'd set up an ambush from behind hedges; one of the big ambushes was away down in Cork, away near Skibbereen and that's where Michael Collins was killed himself. There you'd throw it [Mills bomb] immediately. Because I was in the Reserves I went in for everything. I had no more wit, I should've maybe not bothered with the Reserves but I was young and impressionable; ready to go on the road all the time. It was a hot summer in 1921, very hot, and we were guarding this building. There was some sort of records being kept in it and they had to be guarded, they'd got some word that they [Republicans] were going to take it over. We'd do this two on and four off, the usual way, and I went out and lay in below a bush outside and had the rifle. I was holding it and I fell asleep, I felt something touching me and I immediately jabbed. It was an old tramp; I nearly killed him only he had an old overcoat on him and a couple of waistcoats and I just pricked him. He said he was only looking for a cigarette and was going to search me.

People in the Reserves were mostly from the North; although there was always very loyal people from the South you see. There wasn't such a big force in the Reserves, a big lot of them were in administration, but then there was this section that I was in, it was all rush, rush. There was quite a few joined up and quite a few of them didn't last long because the type of life we were living in. We were wild and rough enough. At Gormanston, that was in West Meath [County Meath not West Meath], there was a station there, a big platoon of police, a big lot of police there, and on a pay night it was like the Wild West.

My over riding memory is of hunger. You see, an open tender with a central seat both facing outwards and no cover on you, you sit in the back for a hundred miles and you're soaked through. It runs down you see and goes right through. There were some army fellows showed me that if you wanted an inside shirt or a long johns dried, you wrung it out well and put it under your sheet on the bed and lay on it. It took three nights to dry it. The first lot that I sent to a laundry I never got them back, they were lost. Oh it was hectic, the two years was really hetic. Whenever the Truce was signed they immediately disarmed us and we handed in our arms to whatever local barrack and they ambushed us on the way back, not to kill us, just more a display of shots at us you know. You see they [Republicans] broke it [the Truce], they just disregarded it. When you'd be at the Vice Regal, the whole night long you would hear shooting and burning going on down in the city, the whole night long. We were inside the gate, inspected every half hour to see if we were there. Sure they could have shot us if they'd wanted to. Casualties were one in seven. They were very high, higher than in any regiment in the British Army.

McMahon (joined 1919).
In the RIC I was stationed in Dublin. Well, at night, you know, there was some trouble in it but I never was in a row or anything like that. It wasn't too bad, you know, but still they wouldn't let you out in the town or anything. Well, you had to walk round at night to see how things were going on, if things were quiet and everything, to see what people were doing and if there was anything to report. No matter what time it was they'd send you out to investigate. I couldn't say I had any

trouble. Of course I didn't abuse my position; as far as I knew I was respected and everything like that. I was respected.

McMENAMIN (joined 1920).
I was allocated to Training Depot at Phoenix Park in Dublin but then it got over-crowded, that was in April, and then before May was out I was transferred down to the Curragh, Kildare, to a sub-depot there. And then before I had my training finished they opened another sub-depot in Gormanston there, County Meath, near Balbriggan. They were getting a big lot of men at that time, they recruited a big lot of Englishmen and ex-servicemen and all that. The trouble was on then, you see, only not on as big a scale as now; a lot of Englishmen joined then. I was then sent down to County Mayo, to Castlebar, and from there out to Newport, and then out to Clew Bay. I was a driver in the Transport Department attached to Newport in County Mayo. There was a good lot of trouble there, in parts of it. Westport, the next station to us, was very bad and we had a few killed in the station I was in too. Shot down by an ambush. We'd a fellow called (....) there, he was stationed out at Navan, round there and they broke up the Barrack, and just a couple of days after in our Barrack he was shot dead, shot dead; and the District Inspector he was shot in the ambush. I was in it too, of course I come out unscathed; he was shot, lying wounded, next to me. It was out on the mountain, and he asked me could I get a bicycle and get a doctor. I seized a horse. Parts of the county were very bad, but we hadn't a resignation at all, not one. There was one or two, they were growing old, who went out on pension. There were a big lot of young ones joined at that time. Well, the Barracks I was in was attacked and then we had a Barrack attacked just up the road. There were several killed there; there were four killed in one night and there were nine or ten killed in another there. Oh it was very bad. There wasn't a resignation in the whole county I was in. No, unless the ones that were going that had thirty years of service or something.

I was driving, I tell you, all the time, I was driving patrols away; we had out-stations. Where I was stationed we had a station at a place (.....), we had a Barracks out there, a sub-station, and we had another on Achill Island. There used to be three police posts on Achill Island. They were looking for drivers and I used to have an odd go at an old car in the country, so I put down my name for it and that was that. There was supposed to be so much on the heads of the drivers in the RIC. We never thought anything about that. It wasn't as bad as now, you know. Ah no. We used to go down the town and have a beer there and, well, you'd be unlucky if you were caught out. Generally speaking, you see, the people of County Mayo were very, very good people; they wouldn't have give you a drink of water, you had a drink of the cream, the top of the milk. Aye, oh aye, very, very good; the ones that weren't in the IRA or anything like that. Generally speaking, you see, in the quieter places, they were very good, you know. They were crying when the police were disbanded and were leaving the towns. A sergeant of the police, they all went to him for everything, nearly, he was the chief adviser and all like – even in 1921 and 1922.

Mostly our patrols were searching out for the IRA and so forth. I remember our District Inspector had one seizure of poteen while I was there but they were actually looking for firearms when they found the poteen, they found the poteen in a hay stack or a straw stack. If there was any crime it was very little. There wasn't very much crime anyway, except the troubles. Parts of it [County Mayo] were very peaceful, you know, and quiet, and other parts of it were rough enough; Westport and Newport, to a lesser extent, and then round the west there, Galway and all round there, you know, a good bit of trouble in it. Donegal [where he was born] was fairly quiet up to that, but they had trouble among themselves then after the Free State was formed; they shot a few just two miles from home. They shot a policeman then. You see, up there, you know, where I went to school, even then they were mixed at the school that I was at. The youngsters used to all meet there and play together and everything else. We had the best Protestant neighbours, you couldn't find better anywhere in the world.

Mayo was a great county there, we used to have to run round Achill Island and all there. It's connected to the mainland by a bridge, they open it up for the boats to come up and down. Oh it was fine county to be stationed in, lovely away out there. It was stormy one day on the island, we had the biggest storm ever, it was a hundred and seven miles an hour there away right out on the coast of Mayo. I enjoyed it at that time, I didn't mind you know, but you see it's really not a job for a policeman, the rifle, the machine gun and everything. No you'd be far better if you had just an ordinary civilian police force – no guns, no nothing at all. It's really not a job for a policeman to have to come and poke round with a rifle while looking for information about somebody breaking into a house or something. You can't do the two jobs.

I did have a very close shave, the top of the crown was hit by a bullet, but you never thought about it. You thought more about it after [disbandment] because you didn't know where the right place was to go you know, a big lot of them went to England. You didn't know what way, you couldn't go home. There was a few of them shot. I thought it was pretty tough then.

STERRETT (joined 1921).
I was allocated to a place they called Queen's County, there was

Queen's County and King's County and the place I was stationed was Abbey Leix. The foot patrol was on when I went to Queen's County, we went out, there was ten of us, five pairs, ten yards a distance. When we were coming out on patrol where the barrack was it was a hollow, a very bad place and there were two big (....) outside and covered with trees. They [Republicans] fired and they missed the first volley, and of course as soon as they fired we fell flat. The Head Constable and the sergeant were at the front, he was very nervous, and he went inside, there were sandbags all round but he got inside and he forgot about us outside, and then they were firing out from inside the Barracks. Then he says, 'oh you should be careful boys, the patrol's outside'. But anyway they chased them off and there was no casualties. All we could see the next day, it was dark then, all we could see the next day, was empty bullets.

When I was in the Depot I took ten days leave and came to Belfast. In the meantime I was allocated to a place they call County Carlow, a small county. And when I was on holidays there was a man allocated in my place, and he was shot dead. He went with a despatch to Dublin see, they must have followed him and shot him dead. I said I was lucky, it could have been me. Well I went down there [Queen's County] and whenever the truce came people got very friendly then, they got very friendly you know. There was another thing happened. They used to make trenches on the road to make an ambush, and cover it over so as what they call a tender would go into it. This girl came along on her bike this day see, and didn't she go into it and break her neck, broke her neck, young, and a nice girl too. The trap was laid for us. It was a nice part of the country down round there. We used to go out on patrol, the police were all out on patrol and walked around. Oh they talked to us then see. Oh they talked to you then for they knew they were only just killing time.

We done patrols at different times, a four hour patrol, and then you done a night patrol in turns. There was a station sergeant there, and he had forty years service, and you'd have thought he was going to live for ever. He was terrible regimental and us about to be disbanded. He was terrible regimental; he detailed the duty. Well then you paraded for the DI to be clean, he inspected your rifle, he inspected your uniform, looked all round you and this fellow said, 'the DI's looking at everything fairly sharp'. The District Inspector says, 'did you shave this morning?'. He says, 'yes sir'. 'Well the next time you shave stand a little closer to the razor.' He knew he was telling him a lie. Ah well it [discipline] eased off. You see if that had been normal he'd have been charged. There was a DI there, they called him Dusty, he was a great man on dust and the fatigue men would go round clearing the place dusting everywhere. You were able to go out then, after the

Truce was called you were able to go about. Anyway they come to me one day and says to me, 'there's a clergyman at the door wants to see you'. 'That's my clergyman at home', I says. So anyway he invited me out to the Manse see and he had a nice daughter so I got very friendly with her, oh they were very nice, they treated me very well indeed, but I wasn't able to go out till the Truce was on. At that time I hadn't a bicycle but there was plenty of bicycles there for me, the old timers there you know. Oh certainly, take a bicycle when you need it. Then we used to go with despatches, three or four of us with despatches on bicycles.

We only had one ambush, that was the only one. Not a terrible lot. Tipperary and these places was far worse, Tipperary was a bad place. But you had to be careful because of these trenches, you'd get to these trenches and they'd be waiting for you, but anyway when it comes to the bit we hadn't very much trouble. People were very friendly, of course we didn't see much of them, the trouble was on and you weren't out. You went out along with the patrol and yarned to this one and yarned and talked to that one you know. They were all very friendly when it come to the bit, very friendly. Queen's County was a good county. Great farming county, good land. Quite a difference from Donegal. Part of Donegal, East Donegal now is a very prosperous place, very prosperous place. It's nearly all Protestants, very prosperous place. At that time there was big families, and they couldn't afford to bring them up you know, ridiculous. There wasn't many jobs about and if a girl got a job she was working for buttons, but it was so hard to get a job you couldn't say a word; or maids, a lot of them worked as maids see, in a house, for next to nothing just. Oh times was hard. I wouldn't like to see them times again.

We thought we were very lucky getting Queen's County. We used to be in the Depot and there were old timers there, they kept so many in the Depot for to keep the place in order. 'Bill', he says, 'you're a lucky man getting Queen's County, you're getting a good county, not much trouble there'. He was right too. Well you had to take your chance, or hope you wouldn't get Tipperary or any of these places. But I tell you one thing, there was a fellow in the Depot with me and he was from Tipperary, and the IRA told him not to join the RIC. But he did and they followed him, for they knew he was allocated to a place called Letterkenny, that's where the Headquarters was for the police in Donegal; they followed him there and shot him dead. The RIC at that time was mostly all Catholics, there was nothing else for them here.

SULLIVAN (joined 1920).
My first posting was Banteer in County Cork, then I was moved to Kantork. All we did was guard work. We were fresh from the Depot and

we didn't know anything according to the older hands there, and you'd feel humiliated when you went into a room and the men would call you a 'Red Shirt' because you were just a recruit. But it was more good fun than bantering. We guarded the surrounds of the station. It was a house set out on its own on the side of the road. I was moved to Kantork to strengthen the station. From Kantork I was moved to Newmarket to strengthen that station. I saw no IRA activity. I heard plenty, for instance, outside Newmarket there was (....), he was a very active member of the IRA and we got assistance from the military. And on a search sure enough they discovered the boy, and a soldier with nearly a rifle as tall as himself caught him. How the devil he got him tied up with his rifle I don't know because he was that small.

We got on very well with the locals, we were able to get bread, potatoes and milk, those were the three essentials; we were able to get them from the locals. A woman kept a jug of milk for us for every day in the week. It was the time of the big pound notes, and I paid her for I was messman. I found that I'd given her a five pound note in place of a pound note – the two were nearly the same size – so when I went back to her she says, 'I have it here'. She just put her hand up on the dresser, took the note out of a long jug and there was my five pound note. You'd get maybe a machine gun attack or something but it was nearly all rifles; there was no machine guns worth while. The trouble didn't worry me. There was a lad with me in Banteer, a fellow named (....). Strange to say he got to be governor of the local gaol here. When in the RIC he used to go out nearly every morning after parade time and he went up to the railway station in Banteer. There was high ground looking down on the station, and there was a volley of shots fired at him, he started to run and there was a gap in the wall surrounding the station and he was going through that and he tripped and fell; that saved him. He didn't get a scratch.

I didn't see much trouble. There was only two instances in Banteer. In some stations it might have led to [resignations] but in ours it didn't. We knew we were on the way out so we were just abiding by it. Although, in Banteer it was like living at home, the people were all friendly. Strange to say there was no demonstrations when we were being disbanded, at least I never saw any. There were no demonstrations of any kind. I was in Coleraine [in the RUC]. I found it great. Maybe walking up the street on my own and the next thing I'd hear was 'hello', 'hello', 'hello' as the people were passing me. In County Cork you just fluffed your way through the streets as well as you could without drawing any attention.

CHAPTER 8

Policing the troubles: the Northern experience

BRITTON (joined 1918).

After training they sent me to Killyleagh [County Down]. That was my first station. Killyleagh was a Protestant area. There was a good few farmers in the area, but a lot of Roman Catholic people worked in the mills. I came to County Down from the Depot and of course I was sent to Downpatrick, that's Headquarters for the county. They told me that I was going to Killyleagh, so I came out in an Irish jaunting car and I thought it a beautiful place, coming out sitting on the side of a jaunting car it was a lovely place. I went out the door and all those wee islands and all, and the sea was in it's full tide, it looked beautiful. I can remember it yet, and I left it in the same jaunting car.

The older cons told you those people who were likely to commit crime, but life was very easy going. You went out there on patrol unarmed. All you had was a baton and handcuffs; you had to carry them but we didn't get issued with revolvers until 1920 I think. Well then, of course, we had the carbine, the Lee Enfield carbine all the time; you had to guard it all the time, it was always lying in the guard room, or day room as they used to call it, and your rifle was up there, the door was open, anybody could walk in. I was in Killyleagh until disbandment. But at disbandment I was transferred to Dundrum.

I was never very busy. There was a sergeant and four constables and you done one day every fourth on guard at the station. You done that for 24 hours. But then of course you could sleep. You slept in the guard room. You brought down your bed at night, well then you slept during the night in the guard. And you kept patrols. You did two patrols in the day. Well then at 9 o'clock in the morning you had to parade. The guard didn't parade except when he attended school. Well then you had a school after that taken by the sergeant on Acts of Parliament for probably about near to half an hour. Then you went out. You might get out in the morning patrol, you see. You're out about 10 o'clock or so, 10 to 1. You patrolled the country by yourself. Well on the night patrols there were two, looking for ordinary crime, just anything at all. I don't think there was any sheep-stealing, there might be an odd house broken into but that seldom occurred either. They were all law-abiding. The only time you'd come to Belfast if you had a prisoner to take to prison, but not very often for there was very little crime.

There was very little fishing. There were two linen mills and they employed a big lot of people around the whole area. There was spinning in Killyleagh, there was a village out about a half mile or so from the town. There was spinning there too. The nearest big house was Killyleagh Castle. There was a Colonel (....). I don't know what he was. He must have been at one time a landlord, I would think. We had very, very little to do with him. Ah, he was a very nice man. He was an old man, probably up in the eighties when I went there, but everybody was all very nice.

There was always something to attract the attention on patrol. And then you probably met somebody you knew and had a yarn with them. I knew everybody. I had to patrol out the country. We looked for anything that cropped up, lights on bicycles, lights on cars, there was very little cars there then. If it come under your notice you would deal with the IRA, but it was basically looking for lights and things like that. You had to be strict with people. Oh, you had to be. If you saw a car coming you probably wondered what he was doing out there at that time of the night. You might go out at 12 and you did to three o'clock. About three hours that was the length of the patrol then, and you'd come back and report. There was no poteen or anything like that. Well I know there was one time, it's a long number of years ago. Comber [County Down] had a distillery in it and this man had a still of his own and you see there was no smell because the smell was from the distillery. He was making his own. But they sell it to publicans. It was quite clear then, clear as crystal, they dyed it brown with tea. They'd sell it then, of course, cheaper than the public house could. I can't remember doing any searching for poteen in Killyleagh.

We did a search once, but it was a house broken into and his gun was stolen. It wasn't the IRA, not in Killyleagh anyway. Life in Killyleagh was very quiet. Well I suppose the people were busy working in the mill, and I suppose they were glad to have a job and that was that. Not much opportunity for crime I suppose with long working hours. I remember when I went to Killyleagh first, the sergeant had two children working you see. Those boys went out at half five in the morning and worked from six to eight, come back then and had their breakfast, and got their dinner hour and worked to six o'clock in the evening, so it was a long day. There was no eight hour day then. There wasn't a problem with drink. I think they hadn't the money, you know.

I must say about them they were very law-abiding. Except you might have a drunk, you know, maybe once in a month or so, or you might have a light on a bicycle or a cart or something. But that was all the crime, with the exception of that one house that was broken into, during my time. What you did depended on their attitude, more or less. If they start to abuse you or if they're not pleased, well then you let the magistrate decide. But relations were very good. There was very little IRA activity in County Down at that time. I thought I was lucky getting to County Down at all, that I wasn't sent down South. There was eighteen of us in the squad that had joined the same time and we trained together. There was only two of us came North, they all went South and West.

I was doing elections in 1918. They took a lot of the Reserve Force and the recruits, the senior recruits, and sent them out in the country to do duty at the elections. I was with a number of others sent to Waterford, so I thought that I hope I'm not sent here. It would take you nearly two days going to Donegal at that time. I think being a recruit I suppose I was kept in Barracks [at Waterford] on reserve. And then I came back to the Depot and continued on for six months of training. Well then at the end of six months there was a shooting took place down in Tipperary. Two of them. There was two of them sent with a horse and cart with half-a-ton of explosives to a quarry and they were walking along, I suppose they had their rifles with them, carbines or whatever you like to call them, and they were ambushed. Two of them shot dead, hadn't a heart – O'Donnell and O'Connell, two very Irish names. The Reserve Force was sent out to this. They kept the senior recruits a month extra to do guards and things in the Depot. But in the North there was nothing like that at all. Practically speaking, very little.

I never had to fire a shot in Killyleagh but everyone fired a practice course once a year. They attacked Crossgar [County Down] with rifle fire, the police station was a terrace house. Well they went into both houses beside the Barrack and tried to blow it up. They couldn't, they weren't well up in explosives. Then they were trying to get in the door, they were trying to open the door. The man on guard shouted; the rest of them were all upstairs. He shouted that they were trying to get in, so the sergeant he came down the stairs to see but he could do nothing so he went up the stairs and a bullet came bursting through the door and struck him in the back. It went right through and come out through the pocket with his keys in. One of the other men came down and carried him up and bandaged him upstairs. But he got alright. The attackers disappeared. They mustn't have been well up in explosives because instead of blowing up, it blew out. They did the same thing at Ballynahinch. It went off but it went out. Well nowadays, you see, they're being trained. They weren't up to the standard they are now in the use of explosives. Well then Castlewellan was also attacked in RIC days.

Support for the IRA in Killyleagh was very little. I don't know of any except the one; he wasn't a native of Killyleagh even. Very peaceful. In the summer time we used to go for a swim in the sea. Maybe if you were guard and wanted a swim maybe one of the other men would take your place for the time being. I remember I was in every day, had a swim every day in my spare time; that was 1921, it was a lovely summer. We were all Irishmen, we were all from the country.

CROSSETT (joined 1920).
Well then the trouble got worse, especially down in the South. But we, the Unionists of us, we didn't let them away with it, for if they shot three police, they shot three police in Ballyronan [County London-derry], you see, well we went and shot three of theirs, do you see.

GILMER (joined 1919).
I was there [in Derry city] for the riots in 1920 but they were nearly settled then, and I was then shipped out to Maghera. It was very stiff [in Derry], you would do eight hours and there were a lot of sergeants there to supervise you. You had to do it but the thing was easing off at the time and then they sent us out to our stations, and I came to Maghera. There were only four men in it [the station] and I think three of them were there temporary; they were all transferred away. That is one thing I'll say about the Maghera folk, they were the most decent crowd ever I worked with. This was the best station ever I was in. The station had the gable-end blown out of it, and there was a lot of them boys outside dead, they were IRA men.

We were mostly looking for poteen. It was a terrible place for poteen and illegal fishing. There was a time, I had thirteen gaffs in my possesion, I seized them all, but strange to say with all my seizures I never got a fish. There was usually only one policeman patrolling for the fishing, unless at night, there was two. There was a big farmer, ah, he was about six foot high, he was a terrible poacher in the river. This one day I went out, it was market day. I sees the man down the river and I saw him taking the gaff. I got him and I told him I was going to search him, and he wound the stick round my head and struck me. I did my best with him, he was taller than me, and he was winding and twisting to hit me, you know, and I put my hand in his pocket, in his trousers pocket, and didn't the gaff run into his leg.

There was one Christmas that the sergeant was on holidays and I got a lot of information. I got six captures of poteen that Christmas. I got information from a lot of them. The parish priest, you know, was good. There was one case in Maghera district, a fellow had a farm and he was terrible at the poteen; I used to search him several times in a week when I met him at night just to put him off it. I got a barrel of wash once just in his fields and I was watching him for a while. I thought if I sent him to gaol he'd be dead nuts on me for sending him to gaol. Father Hegarty was coming along the road and I told him all about it. 'Well', says he, 'leave it me and if I'm not able to do anything with him I will leave it to you then'. He scared the man a bit. About three or four days after a young fellow come off the mountain and he passed me on the footpath and he says he wanted to see me that night. I was afraid of the IRA but at all events he told me to come in plain clothes. It was Father Hegarty sent him, a man was making a still. He was very anxious about them doing it and he wanted to get rid of them. There was one case, it was on the side of a mountain. The farm was on the left hand side. There was a still going in the fire and the children were in the kitchen and they were supping the poteen as it dropped. I started and got the still on the kitchen fire and emptied the wash, but I let a little drop of the wash down and it caught the fire, and man it blazed up just, and I had a fine overcoat on me and it burned the whole wool off it. It was near burning the house but at any rate I got my man and got my poteen and all.

There wasn't much crime around Maghera. There was very little of that. You know, in a police district which gets the name of being a bit tight on them, people put lights on [vehicles] all the time. Markethill was bad for IRA activity. There was a sergeant and a constable shot in Ballyhorn [possibly means Ballymoran] and two nights after there was a Republican house raided and they were shot too, there was two of them shot there, it was bad all round there. On patrol you'd be searching the people, meeting, looking at them. I hadn't any contact with them myself. There was one chap, he was kidnapped. But the locals were useful, talk a bit. A lot of them, principally the priests, they'd give you information. I were very friendly with them. Relations with local people were good. They would back me or anybody no matter what I'd do, like, they were very good. If you treated them decent and straight and helped them in filling in forms or something you were appreciated. I was still asked to do that. I'll make you laugh, I was only about two months out of the Depot and there came a message through from Cookstown that there were three boys in Maghera and they had robbed all before them going to the fair. There was a Republican, he was farmer, and he had a little drink taken. He was after selling a lot of cattle and he had money in his pocket and these three boys got into him, but I told him to come with me and I would leave him home. His wife thanked me. He was a Republican, mind you, and he was very nice to me. Relations were very good in Maghera.

Other features of policing political violence

Morale of policemen

BROOKES
Violence didn't put me off. No one in our district resigned, no one, not one. Morale was good all round. There was one station about five miles away from Ballyduff, a place they called Tara and one day they were bathing and the IRA attacked them in the water. There was one fellow ran right for the Barracks, nothing but bathing pants on, right up the path to the door and he shouted 'open the door'. It was a bit of a laugh that. In Dungarvan some police were taken prisoner and then shot. There was two, they had their hands tied and the revolver was there, and they said they wouldn't tell them anything till they loosened their hands. One fellow drew the revolver and shot the IRA, and then they shot him and the other fellow too. But it didn't put us off.

CRAWFORD
You see the force was largely composed of RC [Roman Catholic] policemen, well, you could count one Protestant out of five. The troubles begun really in 1916 at the Rebellion and from that on it never returned to normality. It didn't put me off from joining, and I wasn't worried a bit about attacks on the police. Oh, the discipline was very good and very high. The discipline never failed, no, it did not. We were determined to see this thing through. There were no resignations in Navan, but I understand some did occur in other parts of Ireland, none in Navan.

CROSSETT
The trouble got worse, you know, but no, it didn't put me off. I was afraid of nothing nor never was. I had no fear in me at no time, went into ambushes when everybody else was panicking, I never seen any reason for fear. That would have been the last thing.

DUNNE
Well, it did lead to a loss of morale. A lot of these fellows, young fellows resigned. I never. I was a sort of fearless type of gentleman, whether I was right or wrong but I never knew any fear, you know that type. I never thought of resigning.

McIVOR
Morale was very high. Ah it didn't reduce it. A man in a wee country station, some of them were away in the fields, away from civilization

nearly, they must have had tension, aye, where they [Republicans] could surround them. There was one time that they [Republicans] decided on this particular station and very heavy snow come on and they called it the Fenian snow. It completely saved them [the RIC] because they [Republicans] couldn't make their way it was such a heavy fall. You see there was not a big force on it. There was one particular place in Bandon that you had to come out, the windows were all sandbagged up, you never saw daylight, the old oil lamps burning, and you went out through barbed wire and then a sort of a maze back and forwards like that. Unless you knew it you couldn't have got out through it, and that was some little hindrance.

McMahon

I remember there was a man killed, a District Inspector and the poor man, he was only a young man too and he was killed; killed somewhere as he walked from Drogheda to Dublin. He was only trying to do his duty. They didn't make me want to leave, no, not at all. I wasn't troubled. There was only one man I seen killed in five years. It wasn't as serious as it was later on and such like.

The Sinn Fein boycott

Brookes

Ballyduff [County Waterford] was alright. They [locals] were all friendly, and there was just the very odd one that would take no notice of you. In fact you couldn't complain about them. It was the outsiders that would have made the attacks, not the locals. They wouldn't have been involved in anything at all. The boycott had no effect in Ballyduff, not one bit. No trouble getting a pint in the pub. Life at Ballyduff was very quiet. You could have walked down straight through it on your own, although when a soldier went out there was never any less than eight of them, but that was a different thing. You could walk, go down, go into a shop, you could buy what you wanted, nobody interfered with you. It was quite pleasant, glad to see you. We played football there. There was a big farmer and he gave permission to use his field. I had to go and ask him. He said, 'any time at all. Play away, put up your posts and play away'. He was a well-to-do man, had hundreds of acres of land. We'd play amongst yourselves, play Head-quarters and we'd go to Dungarvan or they'd come to us then. No locals. They [the Republicans] wouldn't have it, they wouldn't allow it at all. We had no troubles down there, they only thing was when there was a convoy going to Dublin [on disbandment], taking in rifles, the IRA held them up and took the cars, took all the rifles and ammunition. But the trouble ceased some time in 1921. The less trouble we had the better.

CRAWFORD

Navan [County Meath] wasn't so bad about that, the shopkeepers supplied you. But other places they would not supply you, but had no objection to you going, for instance, to take nine or ten pounds of beef and weigh it and leave the money on the counter for it. They had no objection to that, they wouldn't do the serving, they would put it down and let you commandeer it. But you invariably paid for it. I never experienced any difficulty in getting servants, they were nearly all elderly women that did it. I had no knowledge of any of them having been persuaded to stop. Some of the pubs wouldn't serve, but when the Black and Tans came along they would go in behind the counter and serve themselves and take the food out. People were very good, very good, they were all decent, respectable people in the town of Navan, all that ever I met. I used to go in to dancing classes in Navan, in (...) and that was a mixed gathering, as it should be. I hadn't a bit of trouble in mixing with the locals.

DUNNE

In Kinlair [possibly means Kenmare in County Kerry] we soon done away with that. When the police went in there and they didn't serve us, they weren't paid for it so they soon supplied it to get paid. We commandeered stuff and some places they didn't pay for it. I tell you that soon broke the boycott. I remember the first time I was in Sneem and we stayed in a hotel there, and this morning we went in to get a drink and he [publican] shook his head and he walked away. There was two or three youngsters who had come in to scout, you know. There were some places where they designedly refused us point blank, and the police seized it and didn't pay for it. That soon broke the boycott.

GALLAGHER

There was one time they put on a ban in the public houses. You went into the public house and they wouldn't serve you. We used to go into the public house and we'd a pulled a drink ourselves and pay them. The local publicans didn't bother much about that. There was one day there come a lot of policemen up from Sligo town and they went into the pub and ordered a drink. The barman wasn't allowed to give them a drink. They didn't bother, they went in behind the bar, and most of them happened to be drinking whiskey, they just turned on the tap and filled the glass. They left the tap running and left no money. That ended the boycott. The boycott wasn't affecting us at all.

That was a handy way of ending it. It meant there wasn't a time after that we weren't served. It was a big loss to them [shopkepers and publicans], and nonsense. The police had from time to time, maybe, to change houses for drinking in. I remember this big Republican [who ran a public house]. We used to go in a very odd time for a drink, very odd time, do you see, and we were as friendly with him, and he was the top Republican. Ah, sure you'd be meeting them [Republicans] every day, there were some of them the best of friends with you.

GILMER

Ach, the boycott was not too bad, they didn't do that in Maghera [County Londonderry]; they didn't boycott you in Maghera. We played football with them. Life was comfortable enough. It was similar to my father [who was a sergeant at the beginning of the century]. They would do anything at all for me. As long as you treated them decent and didn't go too hard on them. The troubles didn't have much of an effect. There was one ambush. They fired alright but a sergeant Kelner was with me and Kelner was too wise for them. They didn't see Kelner until he jumped on them. Kelner gave them the best hammering ever they got, they went on their knees and begged of him to let them go.

CHAPTER 9

The Black and Tans

Recollections by Black and Tans

Fails (joined 1920, stationed in County Mayo).
I was born in a place called Rathkeale, that's in Limerick. It was a market town. My father was a policeman. He married a woman from Cork. We were all born there. There was six of us. We didn't seem to mind because we thought it was happy and all like that, we could run where we liked and do what we liked. Of course the living was rough then compared to what it is now. We were moved into the city, my father was transferred into Limerick city; he was sergeant in one of the Barracks there. My father and mother always had a shilling to spare. When I was in the police myself the trouble we'd have with pay; we had got a rise in wages and money was slightly better, but at the time my father's wages fed and clothed us. My father asked for a transfer at that time because we were growing up and they didn't think much of the school in Rathkeale. It was a different denomination, and the Protestant population was small there; the teachers didn't like to come. My father and mother thought it was time we got a bit more education and it would be better in a city. You see at that time there was a big Protestant school in Limerick city.

I left school when I was about 14 and I went into an office in Limerick. Well I didn't do so well there. I got another office job in a flour mill. What the prospective employer did in a great many cases was, he'd get in touch with the local head teacher in the school and say he wanted a boy in the office. Well I was recommended. I was there for over two years and then I joined the army. I thought it was marvellous at that time. I was 17 years of age then. It was during the First World War. I joined in 1917. As far as I remember it was 17 January 1917 and we were sent up to the Curragh camp. I was sent up by train. They kept me back a bit as I was under age and actually one of the Sergeant Majors in the army told me that he knew my father, and if he had known at the time he could have had me promoted. I

100

was under age. My brother had joined about 6 months before me and he was in the Royal Engineers. I was in the Royal Munster Fusiliers. I was in Passchendaele. I had been at home at my father's funeral around 1st March and I was only just back when we were told that we were to go away on a draft to France because they wanted Protestant Munster men there; as if they were any better than anyone else. We were sent up into the line and so on but at this time the Germans were halted, you see, and it was a matter of sitting and holding on to what you had. We were in the second line and of course we were there in case of any other attempt. But they brought in the mustard gas, so I got a dose of that one night and the result was I had to go back to the first aid place. They sent me down the line to the nearest headquarters. I was six weeks away from the regiment and during that time as I recall there was quite a few of them killed.

My father had died and my mother was getting a few shillings a week allowance, and then she had the pension too, and she asked me if I couldn't get out of the army so that I could come home. I applied for what you called sympathetic discharge. This Brigadier, he said the way things were in Ireland now you'd better be here, you'd be as well here until they decide what they're going to do with Ireland. So of course, what could I say, only OK, salute and away. Then the Armistice was signed. Well then, you see, the police were after getting a big rise of pay at that time and it was activated later, and I then went up with two other fellows to join the police. At that time, you see, they were sending all the big men, like, that looked well in uniform across to England on a recruiting campaign. They were promising them this, that and the other, and they were sending them over by the hundreds at night. At that time, you see, there was great unemployment in England, everybody was on short comings and they'd come up in the morning on the boat from Dublin. Some of them only had the suit they stood in. But they didn't like the look of the grub when they saw it [in police camp] and that night they were going back by the hundreds. They wouldn't have it at all. At that time, if I was to tell you the way the troops was fed in the police at the beginning you'd be surprised; you'd have thought you were out in Africa or somewhere. Oh very, very poor.

They had you parading up and down the parade ground in the Phoenix Park day after day after day. At that time when you joined the police you were a kind of an infant, not safe to let out by yourself, especially in Dublin. It was just the same as being in the army. There was a couple of acting sergeants there, men, like, that had a bit of experience of training, and they spent their day training us up and down places. Well, for the first two months when you were a recruit you had to be in Barracks at 8 o'clock. After that you were in Barracks at 10 o'clock. If you wanted any special treatment you had to provide it. For instance, you wouldn't get bread and butter in the morning; you'd get dry bread and in the evening at teatime they'd give you a round of bread. The English people wouldn't have that, they weren't going to be like these people from the bogs of Ireland that put up with anything. They wouldn't have that and they were going back as quick as they were coming over. Eventually they formed a committee and they said what they wanted, something in the line of meat or things like that. So what they used to do was give them boiled ham. That didn't eventually satisfy them either so they opened a new training place at Gormanston camp in County Meath, and they put a sergeant in the Irish Guards in charge of us. They were keen to get recruits from the army, from anywhere. They weren't getting enough Irishmen, and the rioting was starting and the shooting and one thing and another.

The army and the police were very much the same, very much the same. You had to study the Police Code and things like that. You had to know how to account for everything. If you arrested a man you had to account for it, what was he doing, what law was he breaking and all like this. In the army if you run into trouble you shot all round you and that solved it. But there was some rough areas where you just had to do the best you could. At that time, of course, the worst part of the area was Limerick, Cork, Tipperary, County Clare and Kerry. Those were the worst areas. I mean, Cork was burnt to pieces; and then the regular thing to happen was maybe ten or twenty soldiers killed sitting in a truck. First of all when they got motor transport they were 'tin lizzies'. They were a danger because you couldn't get out of them. Then they brought in another, better class of an armoured motor lorry. Things were heating up, and when they got these crowds coming over from England they hadn't enough police uniforms, so they gave us half. Whoever was short they made it up with the military khaki. Well then, the locals, women, of course, called us the Black and Tans. That's where the Black and Tans came from.

Well, at that time I had just two months and they decided that I was to go to the West of Ireland. The trouble was going on there and people were being shot; if you reported anyone to the police you were shot. I wasn't exactly a raw recruit because I had the bit of experience of the army and I could shoot if I wanted to. But they put me, with my rifle in my hands, and the box with the clothing, in the van and they sent me off to the West of Ireland to a place called Castlebar, the capital of Mayo. We went by train from Dublin to Galway and had to change trains. There I was walking about, half and half, half army, half policeman, with a rifle and ammunition. We should have been shot down, you know, but we weren't. I was picked up in Castlebar by the local sergeant. It turned out that he and my father were pals. I remember the County Inspector there was one of these men that the more hardships you had the better you were; he wouldn't even let the men light a fire, and when he sat in the freezing dayroom himself he had himself wrapped up in blankets. I was sent on to a place called (......) that was the District Headquarters of that area.

I was in the Black and Tans. They formed a new Corps [the Auxiliaries] and some some people called them the Black and Tans. They were dressed in army uniform. They weren't Black and Tans in the proper sense of the word. They were all ex-officers and nearly everyone of them had an Military Cross [medal] in the war, and they went out on their own. They weren't supposed to be under the authority of the government or anything else, not of the local government anyway. It was a regular war them days. Sometimes the police wouldn't be outside the Barrack door for weeks, you know, things were bad; there were bad weeks and good weeks.

Some of the Black and Tans were bad enough too, particularly when they had drink taken. There were certain ones that were quite good. There was quite a few got married to Irish girls there. At the same time you were at war, you had to try and make the best of it, and if you didn't kill someone, someone was going to kill you. The Black and Tans took reprisals, they sure did. In County Mayo there was a District Inspector, he was an ex-constable himself, and he was all for working in with the locals. But from the minute that the Black and Tans came on the scene, all the shutters went up on the windows and things like that. There was another time that they sent five Black and Tans to Swinford, and the County Inspector told the DI to distribute them to a station, but the DI wanted to get them out of his place as quick as possible. He was probably trying to calm things down a bit, like.

We did very little, to a certain extent. If anything turned up we still went out, and then we would do night duty. We used to go out on night patrol, like, we'd set off there about 5 o'clock and look for cars that might be in a raid. But some other police didn't worry too much. At that time, there was a lack of turf [peat for the fire], and farmers would go round and cut down trees, whole trees, and bury them. We had to stop them. We had to go out with a big thing with a handle on it and anywhere we saw freshly turned soil we'd be poking down it to get this tree trunk. Using them for firewood wasn't allowed. These were big estates in the West of Ireland, people went there for the shooting or the fishing or something like that, and they had all these trees but the local people were cutting them up. We used to cut them for firewood ourselves mind you.

I never actually had contact with the IRA. You never knew where they were. Now there was one place, I was there for a while until they closed that station. There was a man there, he was in the IRA. It was known he was in the IRA but you couldn't get a case against him, he was too cute for that. Then another time we found a man in the bog, he had been there about two or three weeks maybe. He had been a cripple, at least that's what they said, how they identified him I don't know. We had to go and bring him out of the bog. When I was at (....), that's another local place a few miles from Swinford, and we went out to Kilnavee, there was a report that they fired on the Barrack. There was talk that actually some of the shots had been fired by the Catholic curate there; he was supposed to be a bit of a live wire.

There were certain Protestant girls especially you know, they, when we went to the Barracks for our tea, always made a fuss of us because you were a Protestant and things like that. But things got bad when they began burning and shooting things in the West of Ireland. I wouldn't claim that we shot anybody. A man asked me one time when he knew I was in the army did you kill anybody. Says I, 'I do not know'. You wouldn't know because you would just fire and take a chance and actually keep your head down. Of course certain men can know whether they kill anyone or not but the majority of them they really know very much. You see most of the shooting at that time was done by the IRA from behind stone walls, a ditch or something, and you were on the road going along on your duty. There was nothing to stop them shooting you and you would never know it. There was a place, Westport, and they sent out some people from Castlebar in a car, it was an old model T Ford, which broke down. These four policemen were there in the Barrack doing nothing for six or seven weeks. Eventually the mechanic put it together and the next day the police were to return to duty. They came to a bend in the road and there was a big bank up and when the police car came round there they opened fire and there must have been about seven or eight IRA men. The four in the model T car were killed outright, and a Head Constable had his whole jaw near blown away.

(RES) Did it provoke the Black and Tans to enagage in reprisals?

Well, I wouldn't say that they didn't. We had some tough looking hands; it was a case of who got the first shot in.

(RES) Did you engage in any reprisals?

No. Where I was, up in Kilnavee, in wintertime it is a very isolated place. Although, one day we got up to go on a patrol and there the ditch had been trenched, dug out so that if we had gone out in the dark at night we would have probably been killed. There was a local man not far from us, like, he knew about it and he came up to the Barrack to tell the sergeant not to go out. We were out one Sunday morning sunning ourselves in the front of the Barrack, the sun was shining, and I was inside and there came a crackle of rifle fire and made all the fellows jump. We closed the door, banged the windows, locked the cook out and she was shouting out to let her in. Another time I had to go up to the shop for something or other, and I was on a bicycle. I came down on my bicycle all ignorance and the IRA came marching after me. They didn't know, of course, where I was; I didn't know about them being there until after. But it was one of these chance things.

Without being any boast or anything like that, I just, it was a job and it was the only thing I was able to get, or likely to get, so I just carried on. It didn't affect my morale. There was a man there, he was married. He married in England and he came home and he occupied an old house. At that time you were lucky to have anything. Now someone shot him in the arm with a shotgun. The local postman was picked up for it, although I don't think he did it. But the West of Ireland was generally calm enough, as I say, Limerick, Kerry, Cork, Tipperary were the worst areas. I mean the Barracks were being burned nightly in those areas, and if we had been in those areas we'd have had a much harder time. I preferred to be where I was. Not looking for trouble.

THOMPSON (joined 1920, stationed in King's County).
I was the son of a newspaper editor, and he died when I was a baby. I think I remember him but I'm not sure. It was in Cookstown and he was connected with the *Mid-Ulster Mail.* I went and was brought up with my grandfather and grandmother. I had a sister who died in infancy, older than me. I never knew about that until I was quite well on in years. Grandfather was a farmer. Not a very good farmer, more a philosopher than a farmer, read an awful lot. It was a small farm, fourteen or fifteen acres. I never was asked to do any work; if I wanted to do work I was allowed to do it, and if I wanted to run about I was allowed to do that. In the early days when I was going to school money was scarce, pocket money was practically non-existent. We had an old muzzle-loading gun and I used to use that muzzle-loading gun to shoot rabbits and pigeons and sell them to the local fowl dealer, which provided me with pocket money. I had pocket money when most of the other lads had none, and that started me off in the shooting business.

After school the war was on and I bluffed my age and joined the army. This was the tail end of 1917. I wanted to become a soldier. It was glamorous to me before I joined; the glamour left as soon as I joined. I was sixteen. I was a big lump of a lad for my years. I was there in time for the March push, the last kick of the Germans, when they retreated for sixteen days. That part of it was no fun, I was scared stiff all the time. While I was in the army I attended every class and everything else that they did, talked to everybody that knew anything about anything and read as much as I could get my hands on; read about everything from astronomy to deep sea fishing. My grandfather, he had great books like Dickens, Charles Reade, Alexander Dumas and Shakespeare. He was an unusual farmer. He was a bad farmer. He wore a tail coat and he would have a handkerchief stuck in his pocket, all that sort of thing. He was a gentleman farmer without money. He used to get the weekly *Irish Times*, and he got the *Guardian*, and we used to have people coming in.

After the war, in one of the papers, there was some advertisement for an electrician for the power house. I didn't know how to go about applying, and I went to the local sergeant. He said that for any job like that you have to join the police. I took this for granted. I didn't know, I was an innocent gull at the time. You see, you did what you were told; 'ours but to do or die, ours not to reason why' – you know that platitude. I thought he knew everything so I joined the RIC. This was early 1920.

At that time it was easy to join because they were looking for men with experience in arms, you see, and I had no problem. One of the local policemen told me not under any circumstances to talk to anybody or to ask the way to Phoenix Park. A policeman was the only person that he advised me to ask directions from. I said how would I know a policeman. He said, 'ask a man with the most splendid uniform you see'. Well, now, this was perfectly true. Whenever I got off the train there was a big man standing with his back to me with big, broad shoulders. I said over his shoulder, 'how the devil would I get to Phoenix Park?' He turned round and shouted, 'hey Joe, could you take this fellow up to the Phoenix Park?' It was too near curfew and I had to stop in the North Star Hotel. My bedroom door wasn't securely locked, I propped a chair up underneath the handle of the door and had a look out. The window looked out at the back of the building and I remember below there was a glass roof or something but it wasn't that far down, so I could have dropped out in a hurry if need be. I got up to Phoenix Park and signed in there, and then the first real thing that happened to me was I was handed a long canvas bag a bit over six feet long and a shorter one, and he said 'that's the straw store up there'. This was my bed mattress. Now, when I arrived that day there was a lot of fellows, sixteen or eighteen English boys arrived on the same day, so I was in with a bad group.

Black and Tans was their nickname. Black and Tans were regular RIC men and the reason they got that nickname was they were recruited in such numbers that they didn't have a normal uniform to provide them with. You need two suits of uniform because you could get mucked up in one and need a change, but the boys, as soon as they got the khaki suit along with the black one they immediately switched the trousers, wore the khaki trousers with the black tunic and vice versa. I had a khaki suit and a black one as well and I got the dress suit later on.

The conditions in the Depot were good. I tell you what there was a terrific comradeship. There was a comradeship there that you wouldn't get anywhere else. In the case of the army and in the police you do your day's work and unless you're married and living out, you're still together, that's a family feeling, you know. I was put on duty right away. No drill nor anything like that. You see, what they were wanting was men who were already trained. The first duty I had was Quarter Guard and I remember whenever I was on I was at the gate, there were heavy iron railings out across the front and beyond that was the Park itself. They had laurel bushes, thick laurel bushes, over quite an area. Some time in the quiet of the night I could hear this rustling going on and I thought there was somebody there. After all the talk and all the rest of it, I was expecting IRA men coming up to take a pot shot at me. I had the rifle in this hand by the small of the butt and the Aldis lamp in the other, and when I thought I had located where the sound was I switched on the Aldis lamp. In the dark I had been, but a deer stuck its head out; that's what was making the noise.

I wasn't put off from joining because of the trouble, not at all. No, most of them thought it was a kind of fun. The only thing was that the opposing forces weren't in uniform, you didn't know who they were. Most of the recruits that joined along with me were all ex-servicemen, you see, all used to that sort of life. There had been an ambush and seven Englishmen had been killed and were being brought home. The sergeant in charge of us asked for anybody who was conversant with funeral drill. Of course we all were and I was in this funeral party. We went down to King's Bridge Station and we were lined up along the station by the goods wagons. A fellow from Coleraine, he was an ex-Sergeant Major in the army who had joined the police but who couldn't settle down, he was standing next to me. When we got the orders to 'Present Arms' you know, and then one coffin came out and four policemen carrying it, and another and another, he whispered to me out of the side of his mouth, 'by God, I'm going home!' You know, another seven of them all being taken back.

I was only in the Depot for a matter of fourteen days altogether and then I was sent to Tullamore, King's County, now called Offaly. I didn't care two hoots where I was sent. We did a lot of patrols there, they were all big patrols, never less than fifteen or sixteen men out at a time. They'd take pot shots at you from a distance, you wouldn't know where they were coming from. It's very difficult to pin point the source of a shot. Take one or maybe two shots and then nothing more and nobody is quite sure where it came from.

Ordinary offences were also taken care of. I had no police training and I didn't know much so you went under direction. There was always an experienced policeman with us, you see, usually a sergeant or a Head Constable, and they would direct you what to do. From there I went to Philipstown. Philipstown Barracks had been burned down after being attacked. Again we just patrolled as a group of Black and Tans, well, I suppose police. Black and Tans, that was a nickname that was given us by the hostile public. Well a very peculiar thing happened there. Philipstown was a sub-station, Edenderry was the District Headquarters a few miles away. The District Inspector at Edenderry was a man called Magner and we had a chap, a constable in Philipstown, his name was Reid. They were both ex-servicemen, and it so happened that the DI was a Subaltern under Reid in the army, their positions were reversed. The Head Constable there [in Philipstown] was an old policeman of long service and he was a strict disciplinarian which didn't go down too well with the boys; nobody paid much attention to him. When he got any telephone communications from Headquarters in Tullaghmore or from the DI in Edenderry he would button up his tunic and stand to attention. When the DI would come on inspection, the Subaltern would start and talk to his Colonel [now a subordinate policeman] as man to man and that didn't please him [the Head Constable], he was still standing to attention at some distance apart while they were talking and joking amongst themselves. We were all ex-servicemen except three or four, there was fifty there altogether, all ex-servicemen except three or four old RIC men.

It was the same ribaldry and the same give and take as in the trenches. You could have cursed a man from Hell to Connaught and loved him at the same time, you know. You saw fits of bad temper right enough. I remember a Dutch man. He had been a medical officer with the Black Watch during the war and just couldn't settle down to civilian life, and he was a constable along with us. A lot of them couldn't settle and joined the police. Some of them were the nicest fellows and gentlest fellows you could meet. The Dutchman did a lot of good in one sense. Outside Philipstown there was a little village, and there was a confinement there and the mid-wife was having difficulties. The doctor was invited down but he was away. The Dutchman volunteered to go and assist; the doctor's housekeeper came over to the Barrack, and he made a successful delivery. That got the people on the side of the police, at least a lot of them.

You had no real contact with the community at all. Connolly was the local grocer and we got all our stuff there. When you went there you took what you wanted, wrote it down on a piece of paper, they put the price to it, you added it and you paid it. No conversation. I think it was as much fear of retaliation by the Godfathers as anything else. To give you an example, Connolly's shop was not far away from the Barrack. The dayroom in the police Barracks was on the first floor and there was a Scotch lad, I can't remember his name now, he had been over at the shop. There was a few of us at the window and we were making catcalls at him and jeering as he was coming along, and he was doing similar back to us. Then all of a sudden he just collapsed and we thought that he was acting the fool, he started to wriggle about and hold his leg. He had been shot from the bog, he'd been shot through the thigh very close to the Barracks. I remember once I served summonses, I had one for a woman who had cattle who grazed her cows along the road. It was an offence to allow the animals to wander unattended and I served the summons on her. When I went up to the house she was sweeping the floor and I went through the usual rigmarole and put the summons down on the table. She never stopped sweeping with her long-handled beesom, you know, and she swept the summons off the table along with the rest and went on sweeping. I went out, never spoke. It didn't worry anybody.

(RES) Did it not cause you to wonder what you were doing there?

No. It was a job. I wasn't politically minded. I'm still not politically minded. As long as I'm left alone I don't give two hoots one way or another.

I was involved in a couple of ambushes. There was one in (....) and there was odd shots now and again. One of the times I was on a cycling patrol. It didn't turn out to be an ambush, it didn't work out right. There was a short hill maybe sixty or seventy yards long and fairly steep, and half the way down the hill there was an ash tree. I had an old BSA bicycle with two bars on the top, a big, big angle on the right, and it was a big heavy bicycle. Now they had strung a piece of paving wire between the tree on this side and the tree on the other side and pulled till it was tight and wrapped it round. I happened to be leading the patrol by a few yards, freewheeling down the hill and that caught me across the arms here. If I had been riding an ordinary bike it would have caught me round the neck. Then there was the tree felling, digging holes in the road and digging the road away, and all that sort of thing. There were batches of police went down to Cork on what you call temporary duty, and on the night before we went there was a part of the road which we had to watch in case something would be done on it. We stayed out till about four o'clock in the morning, nothing done. When the transport came for us the next day the place where we had been watching up to four o'clock was dug away. They had been sitting watching us until we cleared away and then got at it. Well, it was easy enough to do because it was boggy ground underneath and what they did was gather up a few of the local boys from farms round about and make them dig a bit.

While in Cork I spent a good part of my time at the Infirmary on the top of the hill, a sort of a look-out post. There was a lot of trouble there. In Cork city we were stationed in Summerhill Barracks and once a month we had a get-together in Union Quay, across the river. There was three of us, we wanted to get back. We weren't supposed to go back in threes, three wasn't enough, you know. You used to go in parties of not less than twelve or fourteen. But we resolved to start back on our own. One of our boys which was in the company was a Roman Catholic, the other fellow, along with me, was Protestant. We were seeing people appearing here and there and gathering ahead of us. He said, 'you follow me', and he took us right through the Catholic church. The crowd didn't expect that.

There was an ambush there and they shot up the Auxiliaries, and dismembered them. These lorries that they [the Auxiliaries] used, carried axes and planks; planks to put across holes in the road so that they could drive over, and axes and cross-cut saws to cut away the trees that were felled across the road. These fellows were shot up and they [Republicans] took the axes and dismembered the bodies, you didn't know which head belonged to which. That was a gory scene. I had the feeling that the old regular RIC men had no experience of this at all, because up until 1916 things had been reasonably peaceful. There was no loss of morale, not that I know of. I've heard of (.....), for instance, who was in the RIC. His mother wrote and wrote and wrote and wrote. She kicked up such a dust that he resigned and came home but it wasn't that he wanted to do.

The ex-servicemen in the RIC, the great majority of them didn't want to be policemen. They used to have schools and one thing and another, schools on police duties and so on. All these ex-servicemen, they had no training as such, they had no schooling as such. Anything that they had was picked up was through the years. But we were regular RIC men. You were just the same as the rest of them, the only thing was that they were men with fourteen, fifteen, twenty years service and there was I with one. That was all the difference. We never considered ourselves as Black and Tans. It was the civilian public that gave us that name. We were all young men, you see, and I suppose in a sense it was quite natural when somebody starts ambushing you, the rest reply. People are like sheep; it's common in a group of men. For the most of them [Black and Tans] it was a settling down period. They all had been soldiers, some of them had a tough time [in the war], but in all honesty I have never yet seen a prisoner deliberately abused. I've seen them when they [prisoners] were obstreperous or violent, being overcome but I've never seen a prisoner deliberately abused; not even those that were known to have done things for which they deserve abuse. You know what reputations are. I'm British, I'm British to the core, I've been British all my life.

(RES) So in other words what you're telling me is that the reputation which they got is undeserved and that there were few reprisals.

That's very like a solicitor's question, that's a leading question. What's your politics? I can say again that I have never seen a prisoner deliberately abused. I have seen them controlled when they were being obstreperous for one reason or another, but we only used as much force as was necessary. I think, in my opinion, that's reasonable. I can only speak from my own experience, there may be men who have seen abuses and any tales of abuse that I have heard of have been from the other side.

Policemen's recollections of the Black and Tans and Auxiliaries

BROOKES
The ones that I joined with were all Protestants and ex-army men. We had Black and Tans later on after 1920. They wore a police uniform just the same as ours, but then there was the Black and Tans [Auxiliaries] that went about in Crossleys and they were all nearly officers that were in the army, you know, and there was no fear in them, no fear in them. They were rough, no doubt about that. They just got somebody that were doing something wrong, they would lift him and throw him into this van and take him away with them. A big lot of them were from England and Scotland, and there was so many alloted for this station and so many for that station. Oh, we got on alright, just the same as ourselves. I remember one occasion where this fellow was drunk and the sergeant took the revolver off him and his comrade said, 'you were handed that revolver and you're supposed to keep it. Nobody has any right to that revolver only you so we'll have to get that revolver off the sergeant'. So they went into the office, the two sergeants were in the office and they went in and they said, 'I want Billy's revolver'. He pulled the hammer back on his own and says, 'do I squeeze the trigger or do I get the revolver?' I stepped in between, he says, 'stay you back, Brookes, I don't want to have to shoot you'. The sergeant wouldn't hand him the revolver. They weren't as disciplined as the RIC, not at all. They were on their own, hurt one and you hurt them all.

(RES) Do you think that some of the things they did made your job as a regular RIC man more difficult?

Oh, no, I wouldn't say that, no, you just passed it by and forgot about it.

CRAWFORD

The Black and Tan crowd were all Englishmen, English and Scotch, you see, and there were a lot of them ex-servicemen, ex-soldiers and ex-sailors. They were a mixed gathering. We were a separate group, kept separate altogether from the Black and Tan crowd. They had already received some kind of training, and they were considered trained enough and they did not require to know any police duties at all because they were primarily concerned in putting down trouble. There were a big number of Black and Tans in Gormanston, and I was there when Balbriggan was sacked, that's only three miles from Gormanston. There was a DI and his brother, a Head Constable, shot dead in Balbriggan. The Head Constable was just after being promoted and he made arrangements with his brother, the DI, to meet in Balbriggan, which was thought to be a quiet enough place down there. They went into a hotel there and had some drinks and probably something to eat, and when they came and were getting into the car both of them were shot dead in the town. That night the Black and Tans broke camp and sacked the town, I think it must have been up to thirty houses burned down that night, furniture carried out and burned in the streets and I expect a lot of looting.

The regular force didn't have much contact with them at all, we didn't really know them, they were stationed along with us in different huts but they were never popular with the regular force. We didn't just approve of their methods of work and you can understand why. I don't think it was the proper way of dealing with it, an emergency like that. You make a lot of enemies and turn people against the police force in general because they put them all down as the one force.

(RES) The actions of the Black and Tans made your job as a policeman harder didn't it?

It didn't make it any easier, put it that way. You see, they were a peculiar crowd. You see that was a reprisal, they went out that night after the shooting, they went out, broke out of camp, they didn't go out under orders at all. The RIC didn't like it, they didn't like it. They were never accustomed to that sort of thing and they didn't like it at all, no.

CROSSETT

I met one or two of them, there was some right fellows and then again there was others who weren't great, weren't good, you know. They would a stole things if they got into a shop there, raiding a shop, you know, put a wedge of bacon in their big coat pocket. Well I didn't like that. A Black and Tan and me, I got hold of him by the two arms like that, but it was a dirty trick. I had the hold of him amd he just put down the head and he just hit me fair there with his head. They'd been through the army and all around, and if they got a drop of drink, like. But then there were some good fellows, there was some used to come and sing in our choir.

Do you know this, that the RIC at one time was the best police force in the world. Because of general deportment and manners, big in height, and their duty; prevention and detection of crime was one of the finest, and the security of people and places. Some of the things the Tans done wasn't nice, that's the truth. But they weren't all bad. We didn't like them, we would have no place for them, we didn't like them coming along and mixing with us.

(RES) Would you think that the Black and Tans made the job of the RIC harder?

They did, I believe they did. Well, something they done sort of pulled us into bad repute, you know, that was the way. I remember a Black and Tan, an Englishmen, they were washing [the station] down, they weren't experienced in gardening or anything, and they were washing down and tidying up, and one lost his temper. He thought that we had far too nice a job out in the garden digging and he come out and give a lot of old snash. We had boxing gloves in the Barracks and we scampered in and they got the gloves on. It went on for a bit till the Black and Tan threw the gloves off, you see, and went at him with open fists. I caught and hit this Black and Tan, I couldn't see this Irishman getting it, and then, of course, somebody else of the Black and Tans come in. Well, such a piece! The sergeant come down and we had a window broken, a panel off the door. Ah, they got the worst of it. We were stronger and bigger men. God, I mind that, it was the greatest, it just brought it to a head, you know, the one was jibing at the other and talking.

Officers of the English army [the Auxiliaries], they were all dressed up, got a pound a day, a revolver strapped to their leg. They sailed round, thought the Sinn Feiners was afraid of them, you see, and scared the life out of them. Ah, we were nothing, we were just the police, the ordinary police. We weren't fond of them, like. We had to stand the brunt, we had to stay there, while they were sailing here and there.

DUNNE
We had the Black and Tans in the station with us, some fine fellows and some damned nuisances too, but the Auxiliaries kept to them-

selves. They weren't in our town, they were in Cork. There was an awful ambush there outside in Cork there one time, there was two or three police officers murdered. The Auxiliaries didn't mix up with the police at all. Some of the Black and Tans were alright, some of them were decent fellows, and some of them were a real damned nuisance, you know. Drink; they were a bit rough, especially when they got drink taken, but, you know, there were some fine fellows among them. They didn't help our job. Well, some of them, of course, weren't fit nor even accustomed to policing. But they started drinking, there was a lot of ex-servicemen, they started drinking very much and then, it went down hill. Reprisals happened too. Of course, there was more than the Black and Tans helped to get reprisals. I remember the police at Tralee coming out and doing a lot of damage to property, it was a protest against our fellows. The County Inspector, he saw that there was some excitement on, and he asked the men not to do anything wrong, but there was a bit of sacking in the town, I suppose, more from frustration. But reprisals were mostly done by the Black and Tans.

FLIGHT

We often went out with them, if they were going to search some place we went out and gave them a hand to help them with the local knowledge. They called around regularly. Well they weren't as well drilled as the RIC. I mean to say, when I was in the Depot in Dublin, like, when you passed out you were a fairly fit man, the training was very good. They didn't take it as serious as the real RIC did. They were fairly rough. Of course the real Black and Tan was the Auxiliary, more or less, they had nothing to do with police Barracks, they had their own headquarters in different places. The Auxiliaries were fairly rough, they done their work in a very rough way, I mean to say, as regards interviewing people who they met on the roads and one thing and another. Of course you couldn't have been wearing kid gloves with the public at that time either. Well, the majority of the Black and Tans were different altogether to the Auxiliaries. The Auxiliaries were in a kind of a world of their own, they raided rough. The Black and Tans, any of them that were with the police in the Barracks, they were just the same as the police themselves. Their discipline was fairly strict.

GALLAGHER

There was some of them in every police Barracks, the RIC men was getting scarce and they brought in the Black and Tans. The Auxiliaries was a force by themselves. There'd be a hundred in the squad and they took over some big house that would accommodate them, in fact they took over our house in the Barrack. They weren't there more than a week till everything was topsy turvy, there was nothing right about it. So the RIC had to supply them with a Head Constable and a constable for office work; there wasn't one of them Auxiliary officers who was a first class scholar. All of them high ranks in the army and no education. The RIC had to do the whole paperwork.

The Auxiliaries were in the army, and they had it rough in the army, so what more could they be? The Black and Tans were ex-army men that they were recruited for the police. A Black and Tan was a policeman; an Auxiliary wasn't. There was some of them right good, like all men of war and ex-army, and some of them mixed. Their atrocities were against [the interests of] the RIC men. They weren't dependable enough. They were the scum of Britain. We could have done without it. There was some of them honest. But I remember one of the Black and Tans was sacked in Dublin and it was no time till he had rejoined under another name. As long as they were ex-army they could join easily. It wasn't like the old RIC, they looked into your character when you joined the RIC long ago. They came out of the army in my time in 1918 and they joined the police force, and they done damn all. They [the authorities] were easier on the ex-army men. If it was one of us, we would get the sack. But there was a good few men in the RIC who joined the army in the First World War, of course, it would be only for the time of the war. They weren't army men at the back of it all.

McIvor
We had no truck with the Auxiliaries at all. They were a force unto themselves, I think they were the ones that got the most hatred really. The were rough chaps indeed. I think they probably made the RIC's job harder. The Black and Tans they weren't as bad as the picture that is painted of them. Of course, if they were ambushed and had a lot of them shot, well then they retaliated. One man, a Head Constable, he took charge of a squad, he was always in plain clothes, never wore uniform, and they had a big price on his head. He was an ordinary police officer, he was ex-army, and they had a thousand pounds on his head dead or alive. But they never got him and he went to Canada, I believe, after disbandment. Well he was on a special squad, he had his men with him four or five of them all dressed like old farmers, they gathered the information. Oh there was quite a lot of undercover work. There was one man along with me in Bandon at that particular time and he was a sergeant and he said, 'I have a sort of a presentment that they're going to get me'. 'Ach', I says, 'sure everybody thinks that some time or other'. And so they did, they got him whenever he come back to Dublin. They shot him coming out of chapel.

McMahon
Black and Tans came in at the end. They were alright to work with. I didn't pass much remarks on them, give them their dues they were

alright, reasonable enough you know, I couldn't say much about them.

McMENAMIN

We got on alright. The Auxiliaries were all ex-officers, nothing below the rank of Regimental Sergeant Major. Oh they were wild men too, they were always boozed up, you know. The Black and Tans got their name at the railway station that was opened in the sub-depot at the Curragh, Kildare. The Black and Tans paraded down at the railway with police caps on them and khaki uniform. That's how they got their name, the Black and Tans.

STERRETT

I never came across them much. The Black and Tans were all English and Scotch people see, and they were rough, but there was two, we had two, they were two gentlemen and they wouldn't associate with the others. They always kept to themselves, they were reading books and all this and they didn't like them because they were very respectable. But the others were very rough, they were very rough, f-ing and blinding and drinking and booze and all. They'd have shot their mother, oh desperate altogether. We had about ten of them there see, but they weren't too bad. There was a couple of Scotch fellows there and they were a bit rough, but these two Englishmen, they were terrible nice fellows.

SULLIVAN

I did meet the Auxiliaries but we never mixed with them. We thought it laughable to see them with the gun strapped to the thigh. We didn't look upon them as enemies or anything like that, but as men that were above us. They were nearly all ex-officers from the army. They did a good job, although in places they got the name of being harsh. You'd get a bad name anyway whether you were good or bad; but I saw nothing wrong with them. They were separate, they worked different altogether from us.

CHAPTER 10

Disbandment

BRITTON

Well I was fairly keen to go [to join the RUC] because at that time ex-RIC men who went to their native place were shot dead. On disbandment a lot of them went to Dublin when they evacuated all the Barracks. The man that was leading a group of cars took the wrong road, there was an ambush waiting for them on the road that they should have taken. Another man told me, he died here just about six months ago, 96 years of age, he was stationed in West Cork. After that they didn't want to put them on the road and so they put them on a boat in Cork to ship them up to Dublin. It was stormy and there wasn't one on the boat that wasn't sick.

Well, I thought I'd be safer where I was, and then we were armed at that time. From about 1920 or 1921, they were very hostile specially in the South and South West. I knew a chap, he went home, it would be in May. He went home to County Monaghan and they raided his place, but he got out. He had found them and hid in a garden of potatoes. He hid among the potato tops, then made his way into the North. The Palestine gendarmes, I'd liked to have went there too at disbandment, so I applied. I sent in an application. Refused. They wanted me to stop in the North. They were anxious, very anxious to get me to go to the RUC. The District Inspector come out to give us a lecture on it and asked us if we would join. There was a chap down in Tipperary, there was two or three that I knew well, and after a while they came up here and joined. Some went to Palestine and they'd a very good time. A lot of them came back and rejoined the RUC then and they got their service in the RIC to count. They couldn't go back to their own homes because they'd have been shot right away, so like for safety, they joined the RUC. The only Roman Catholics that would join at that time was the men that were in the RIC.

BROOKES

They [relatives] had a job for me in Canada and then that Wall Street crash came and the millionaires hanged themselves and jumped out

117

of windows, and all sorts in America. Canada was in a bad way. Canada as well as America, and just didn't know which way to turn. This job was picked out for me, my brother was in it, and he was fairly well up and he got this job for me but then this all happened and it just fell through. I was transferred [on disbandment] from Ballyduff back to Dublin then, Ship Street. The morning we were transferred we looked out and the yard was covered with soldiers, you'd have thought the whole British Army was there. They escorted us by train from Waterford and then we got in a destroyer and went from that till Dublin in the destroyer. All the stations was closed down, everything was handed over to the Free State. On disbandment the RIC remained a disciplined force. The RUC wanted men from seven to fifteen years service. Well, a man that has fifteen years service he has twelve years added to it, and he has nearly a full pension and he says why should I go to Northern Ireland and risk my life for that. They had to take the younger ones, with two years service. I never had any desire to go to Palestine. I didn't like the thought of it, there was that much happening there at that time in Palestine.

CRAWFORD

I was in Navan till the Barrack closed, till the station closed, and I remember our boxes were taken out onto the street and we were sitting on the boxes waiting for lorries to bring us up to Gormanston. I remember the Barrack being taken over and as we were sitting on the boxes outside the first thing I did see was the Tricolour hoisted over the Barrack door. I understand afterwards, I heard this, now, but I can't vouch for it, that the party that took over the Barracks had no authority at the time and were put out by the Free State troops afterwards. But when we left it the Tricolour was flying over it and we went on up into Gormanston. In Gormanston we went on with the usual work of the police. Well, I was disbanded from Gormanston, they paid them off at the rate of about a hundred a day. Well, the big majority were from what were called then the Free State, you see, or the Republic, like myself. They just could not go home there, lots of men went away and joined the Palestine Police, some of them went across to England and joined the English police, some of them went to America but very, very few went home to their native place. They had to go away because some men after going home were shot at for going home even though they were disbanded and out of job. A lot of them went to the Palestine Police. I went back to Monaghan but I was warned to leave it; and I did leave it. In Monaghan at that time the regular RIC were gone, the army was gone and you had no protection.

I got warned by a man who knew what was going on in IRA circles and was friendly enough to pass the word. I cleared out and went along and walked the railway line until I came into the North of Ireland from Monaghan. I had my name down for the Palestine Police but I wasn't called at that time. Then I went on to Portadown and I contacted a policeman whom I knew there, a Donegal man, I knew him well and he advised me to go and join the Special Constabulary. He says, 'there's no good you knocking around here playing larkey, go into Armagh and join the Special Constabulary until such times as recruiting opens for the RUC'; which I did. I had to start the training all over again. I was promoted sergeant and sent out with a platoon to the border, to Newtownhamilton on the Castleblayney Road, just on the very border and there we had to patrol, day and night. I put in an application for Palestine but then (.....) when I joined the Specials and I heard no more word about it. A big number of the Southern fellows put in applications to serve in the North, came North and rejoined the RUC whenever they were accepted. Any of them that had, you see, the twelve years, there were twelve years added to each man's service for the purpose of pension, well any fellow that had twenty-eight years' service, he took the full pension of 30 years, twelve added, and he went. He was happy and content and went away to look for another job, went to America or somewhere else and he had his pension. Well, then, nearly all the short-term men put in applications to come up North, and some of them went to the Civic Guards as drill instructors and training. There was at least one District Inspector went to the Guards and remained on in the Dublin Depot, and he used to be a DI in Monaghan, one time, and he went to the Guards Depot for a long time. It were RIC men that trained them and schooled them. They were safer there than going home, they were safer in the Depot.

CROSSETT

I was discharged off the police and came up to the North here. They [Republicans] shot three policemen down there in Ballyronan. Well I was only up from Tipperary and they come out and asked me would I go down and reinforce the Barracks under the auspices of the Specials. So I picked up two men and I went down straight away into the trouble again, as it were, where the three men were shot. No, there was no fear in me, I never was afraid of any of them things, it didn't bother me. We hadn't as much to put up with as what they have now, and the civilians were helpful. A policeman's no good if the citizens are not working with him and ready to inform. I remember one time a girl come up to the Barracks and told me, I was going out to see a wee girl out the Longmore Road, you see, and she said for to not go out this evening. So I told a neighbour, one that I could trust, to see if anybody would come along at that particular time, and right enough she was telling the truth.

Some got a chance of going to Palestine. I had a wee pension, you see, heard about this wee pension and I thought that I would make sure that I made no blunders and I went nowhere. I just settled for coming home and taking the wee pension. Some of them went to Palestine, some of them joined the Garda, and we got a whole lot of them come up to Ulster here. We got some money when we left the police for having to go away maybe to Scotland or England or somewhere when you couldn't go home. They gave you some money for to get you away from trouble when you were disbanded. Sergeant Connor was with me, he was in Cloughjordan, down in Tipperary, and then he was stationed in Cookstown, he joined up with the RUC. I wanted no police. I tell you, if I had been put down to a real exam, I wouldn't a passed it here, you see it was a cut of luck that I got in. But I joined the Specials. Our locality was predominately Protestant, you know, but even the Catholics were just as good friends to me, all the time, even yet. There were nobody intimidated me. I remember I was on the B Specials here and there was two men come to me and they told me that I should quit. Says I, 'I think I'll not bother', and there never was another word about it. We done our drill up in the hall, in fact we done our drill in the local hall surrounded by Roman Catholics, and some of them come in at night; we would a been practising this military shooting, and some of our Roman Catholic neighbours, we were good friends, you know, they would come in and watch us. (....), he had got a bottle of stout or two and he wanted to get shooting, you see. So we let him get a shot or two. What would you want better than that? There was three of them, but like they were good, I always kept on good relations with everybody.

DUNNE

I remember sometime before that Kinlair [possibly means Kenmare] had been isolated, the railway lines had been pulled up and there was no provisions coming into the town, in fact the town was nearly in starvation, and finally a boat came in from Cork with provisions. It arrived at the pier this evening and, of course, the crowds went down to see the boat coming in. We were on patrol, about six of us, I think, and we went down too. The whole crowd was watching the unloading of the boat. I noticed a couple of men there bending down and youngsters talking to them, and the next thing the crowd started to disappear from the pier. I suspected that there was something wrong so we walked off too, among the crowd, and as we came down to the square we were fired on from an old burned down courthouse. The courthouse was burned down and bullets started to fly round. We returned the fire and the military were at the top of the town and they thought they were fired on too. They opened fire down on top of us.

I don't know how we escaped. There was one man wounded. I think he was an innocent civilian but it was just as well they didn't get us down in the pier anyhow.

We were sent to Naas, near Dublin. In Naas things were natural, we used to do the beat just the same as we did years ago, and after some time then we were sent up to Gormanston which was a camp in County Meath, there was hundreds of police in there waiting for disbandment. When we got into the Depot I was attached to a crowd to break up stations, take the police up from the country to the camp for disbandment before handing over the Barracks to the Free State. You knew it was coming to an end, but at the same the discipline was still there up to the last I remember. I remember being on duty at the Gormanston camp when the Cork City Police Force came in for disbandment, oh, I suppose there was a couple of hundred of them. I'll never forget as they came in that gate, they came from Cork to Dublin by boat, and I often thought, you know, such a fine body of men, there was hardly a man under six foot and they came in, swinging in that gate, and inside two weeks they were scattered to all parts of the world. I thought it a shame, you know, such a body of men to be, you know, being paid off and nowhere to go.

I applied for the North. Well nine of us in my batch applied for the North and we arrived in Derry on 16 May 1922. On our way we were travelling in plain clothes naturally, but we had our regulation boxes and uniform concealed in the boxes, and a gentleman came along with a revolver hanging at his side, and he looked into every carriage. Well, now there was nine of us in the one carriage, nine big lumps of men and he never let on to see us and never interfered with our boxes. We often thought this strange too.

I enjoyed the RUC more or less. I didn't fancy going back to civilian life. I didn't think that I'd settle in any other job and, of course, being married at the time you were glad to get a job. I thought this was all I could get. Well, of course, I could go back to the land again, I could go back to the farm. I didn't think I would experience any intimidation, although I went home on leave during my RIC time, and well I saw a bit of a difference. In fact some of my old friends, you know, well, they'd just speak to you and no more. But then that soon died down too; after a couple of years I used to go home regularly.

FAILS
[In the Black and Tans] I don't think that we discussed it [disbandment] to any great extent, it was always something that happened yesterday, somebody killed last night, you see. We might say ah to heck, it's about time they did something with them or something like that, but I had no interest in politics. On disbandment, I couldn't go

home then. When I was discharged they sent me home from Castlebar with all my old equipment, of course we had no guns or ammunition or anything. So to avoid any trouble they got us off the train at a little station on the northern side of Limerick and I got a car to my home. I don't think anybody really knew whether I was there or not, but after I'd gone to Belfast to look for a job, there was some IRA people came wanting to know where I was. Whether I'd have been in any trouble if I had been there I don't know. Some of these young fellows, you know, think it was bravado. I would like to have stayed [at home], but I knew I wouldn't get work there.

They brought up this question of sending a party to Palestine to sort out the almost similar situation there. I forget how many of us went, I think it was five companies altogether at varous places. I was at a place called (......), with another company in Jerusalem and another in Samaria. They were doing, you might say, the same. They had nothing to do with the local Arabs at all. We signed on for twelve months and when it was time for changing, they hadn't any more fixed up so we had to do another month before they sent us home. I didn't like Palestine. It was alright but I can't stand the heat. Now in Palestine when we did a lot of training and marching and things, we'd do nothing else but lie up for the afternoon. I enjoyed that. I never was keen on going out, I always thought it was too hot for me altogether. But it would have been alright, I suppose, for health reasons. There was a man there from Belfast, he had joined the RIC during the trouble and went on to Palestine. He did four-and-a-half years out there. There were bits of riots, you know, the same as in Ireland. There was some of the police there then that knocked them Arabs about a bit. Oh, they were rough, yes.

I didn't join the RUC. My uncle wanted me to join it. My father and another uncle, his brother, was on the police. I was married then, you see, and my wife thought we'd be better off going to America. Her father went there when he was fifty-seven years of age and learned to drive a car in America. We went to America and, of course, at that time there was nothing but the depression, you know, it was upsetting everybody. The only people making anything of it was the Americans. I got started in a typewriter factory, the lowest kind of job you could have. I was about twelve months at that and I wasn't getting on. They introduced short time to three days a week and then I wasn't an American citizen, so I came home.

FLIGHT
I joined the RUC in 1922 about two months after coming off the RIC. At that time things were very sharp around Dundalk, and the next thing I'm going to tell you now, you'll think it funny. Sinn Fein was

actually taking over Dundalk and they were searching trains going to Belfast for to see if there was any ex-RIC men on them. I and two more went to Dublin and took the boat for Glasgow and went that round-about way to get to Belfast to join the RUC. At that time of course, you see, road traffic was light, there wasn't much of a chance of getting a vehicle going from Arklow [County Wicklow] to Belfast. I think it wouldn't have been very healthy to go back to the farm in Wicklow. I wasn't warned but some of the other fellows that were for joining were warned, but I never got a threatening letter or anything like that. I fancied it [staying on the farm] alright but in the end it was not good, but I didn't mind in the least going North.

GALLAGHER
I didn't bother joining the RUC. A lot of young boys joined [the RIC] at the time of the troubles, a good few from around Boho, they left the RIC and come back here to settle down and didn't go into the RUC. They weren't married, were young, single fellows not married men. They had their small pension, a pound a week was money to them at that time. They had seen the shooting in the Republic, and I didn't want to come back into it here.

MCIVOR
We had a section in St. Stephen's Hospital where we had to guard the windows, a whole ward. We did the duty from 3 o'clock in the daytime till 3 o'clock the next day, and when I came back all my stuff was lying on the square and I was completely disbanded. I was disbanded while I was on duty and my stuff was thrown out there. The last parade, they [the RIC] wouldn't hand over to the IRA, or whoever was in charge, they wouldn't hand over, but they handed it over to the British Government, the army. And then they [the RIC] decided that they would have a march on Dublin Castle. There was a man the name of Cope who was the Head of the Civil Service [although Cope was a leading civil servant he was not Head of the Civil Service], and he was going to give them very little compensation, and they took this very bad and they marched, all fell in on the square and decided that they'd march down through Dublin, pull him out and maybe shoot him. The Commandant of course pleaded with them to stop. This was a terrible thing; the RIC never would do the like of that. But they got the twelve years added to their pension. A lot of them [disbanded RIC men] couldn't go home at all, there was one particular sergeant he was at the gate along with me we were going out, he says 'I'll be alright Mac I have a brother in the IRA'. As soon as he landed in Cork they handed him the notice, twelve hours. Out you go. I saw him in Dublin afterwards, he was terribly shocked about it.

After six months I joined the RUC. I was very nearly in Palestine. I filled up everything but I hadn't put in the application when I went to see my uncle in Dublin, who was an ex-RIC man. He says have nothing to do with it. I met some of the boys afterwards and they said, 'weren't you lucky that you didn't go'. They got terrible treatment. Ah a lot of them went to English forces and different other forces.

The Cork force, whenever they were disbanded, the arms of course were all taken off them [when they were] in civvies, and coming up [to Dublin Depot] they were ambushed. They had to go back and come up by boat. In Dundalk, they [Republicans] asked for them [ex-RIC members] to come out but nobody went, so they burned them in the station; very vicious and wicked. They weren't so well armed though as now. There was one particular incident happened in Tipperary, we were brought down to take over charabancs, three charabancs, and these were open seats and a hood, old fashioned ones. The IRA used what they called a flying column; they tore out to one particular place to do some damage and then go back, they could carry quite a lot. I was in one of those [open charabancs] when they attacked, and I was a rear gunner by the way, and I sat up where the hood was, we went over a bridge, a bump, a wee humpy bridge, out I went, landed on my backside on the road in the middle of the night. But luckily some of the fellows looked round and saw me and got the driver to toot and toot the horn, and here I'm coming walking along wih my rifle and a hundred rounds of ammunition, a revolver and a Mills bomb, and the IRA never got me.

On disbandment I stayed in Dublin for a day or two. I liked Dublin, it's really a capital city you know, Dublin. Then I went home. I was sitting on a wall in a wee place called Cullybackey in County Antrim, talking to a fellow, and two police cut through on their bicycles. I recognised one of them; the last time I had seen him was in King's County and I shouted after him, a fellow the name of (.....), he never looked round. I yelled at him again and then he did look round. He says, 'I thought I was followed'. He says, 'I thought somebody was following me and I was afraid to get off'. He come back and told me I should rejoin, he had rejoined you see, and that put it in my head.

McMenamin
You had what they called the Irregulars, that was the out-and-out IRA men, they didn't agree with the Truce for Ireland at all and they kept on fighting the Free State Army. Ex-policemen weren't welcome either. On disbandment I went up and lived in Derry and then my brother he went over to England. I went over to lodge with him; I already had filled in the papers for the RUC. Where I was stopping in

Derry there was a sergeant there, a lot of police dined there, they didn't have any messing facilities in the Barracks. He and I filled up the old forms. Then I was recalled. I come back into the police again, I was only out two months; I went out in August and come back in October. Some of the older men in the RIC burned the application forms [to join the RUC] of the younger ones in order to strengthen their case for a pension. They burned them.

I joined the Palestine Police but I can tell you I didn't go. I was called to report at a place in June 1922, and I went down to get paid off at the Company office at Gormanston. It was there I went for disbandment. But there was an ex-lieutenant there from the army, he was actually an RIC man, he joined the British Army in the 1914-1918 war. There was another fellow there and he was an ex-soldier, the both of them had malaria, they got it out there in Palestine. They put me off.

After disbandment, fellows went back home. I remember a couple of brothers, they were attacked and the house was attacked with gunfire. I didn't go back then to Donegal from 1922 until my mother was ill, my mother had a heart attack in 1924. My other brother that was on the police, he was in England, he come over too.

STERRETT
Whenever I was disbanded from the RIC in Dublin I had a brother on the RIC in Belfast and I came to him. I remember there was a girl and she tipped off my brother to tell me not to go home to Donegal because they were lying in wait for me. The man who was going to have to shoot me, him and I was pals, used to work on the next farm, and he said it was the toughest order ever he got to have to shoot me. That was why he tipped the girl to tip me off. He knew the train I was leaving from Dublin on, I was leaving at 3 o'clock. I didn't know this till afterwards. It was decent of him all the same, decent of him. Well then I was off four or five weeks when I applied for the RUC [and was] allocated to Springfield in Belfast.

Towards the end when you knew you were going to be disbanded discipline got a bit lax, very lax, killing time. We used to go out on patrol and just killing time you know, out round about, you didn't do anything you know. They wouldn't serve police in a pub for a drink, if you went in for a drink they wouldn't serve you; so this fellow, says he, 'oh if you won't serve us we can serve ourselves', and walks in behind the counter. When we were done left the money lying on the counter, he says, 'there's the money for the drink, take it or burn it whatever you like'. They [publicans] couldn't do a thing. There was one man went to the door, we were carrying rifles at this time, and one man went on guard and by that time there'd be seven or eight of us together. The IRA come along and warned them that they weren't to serve us, so of course you couldn't blame them, they'd go in and shoot them. Anyway they [the RIC] went in and says 'we'll serve ourselves', and left the money, didn't pinch anything. Oh it got very lax all over. Sure we were in the Depot there then and it was different altogether from the first time I was in the Depot. When we were disbanded it was different altogether, it was a case of killing time.

I didn't go back to Donegal for a couple of years, I took time to let things cool down a bit, you know. Everybody was as friendly as ever, no bother and they came to the house and all. When you come there in the country you walk in you see, you don't get invited in, you just walk in you know. But a brother told me, he kept me informed see, told me to wait a while and see. Oh they were very friendly with him, they were very friendly.

SULLIVAN

I was moved into Cork city and I did the rest of my time there until disbandment. On disbandment we were marched down to the quay side in Cork and took the ferry to Queenstown and then the SS Lady Wicklow for Dublin. It took us eighteen hours. The railroad men refused to take what was called a body of police. They refused to carry us so we were put onto the ferry and boat. I was in Cork just before disbandment and in several of the stations around the city there was ex-policemen of many kinds. They were back into their own job and they were given authority by the Free State Government, sworn in and all. They'd be taken on as Civic Guards because there wouldn't be trained men. I couldn't join them. I didn't like them just. Somehow I felt at home in the RUC although I was far from home. I thought it better and they were better paid than the Civic Guards were.

I had it on my books to go to Palestine and I just withdrew my application. I realised that Palestine was coming to an end. I'm mighty glad I did because the force was broken up a short time afterwards and all the men that went out to Palestine were sent home. They were given some kind of a pension but I think it was very small. I was keen to join the RUC. Once I was away from home I decided to remain away because what was there to do for me at home? I would be getting maybe a job as a shop boy, about half-a-crown a week. I would be adding an extra mouthful to the family. I enjoyed it in the RUC. The only time I had to draw my baton was during the riots in 1925 [while in the RUC] and that was on the Newtownards Road and it was more of a chase. The only time I used it [a rifle] was in target practice, same with the revolver. Somehow I never liked firearms. To use them went against my grain. I never liked using them. It took me all my time to use them for target practice. I never had to use a firearm for anything other than target practice.

THOMPSON
In the RIC I went to work in the power house at Gormanston camp. I was in charge there and they kept me on after disbandment as a civilian. When disbandment took place, the camp cleared out, everybody went home and I got into civvies. None of the other boys wanted the job. Then they [the new government in Ireland] sent boys from Dublin, and I had to train them into the working of the power house. This lasted after the Free State troops came in. One night an elderly man called me aside and he says, 'I'd be very careful if I was you. I heard the boys talking about the man in the power house being an ex-policeman, and they weren't saying it in very friendly tones'. So I uprooted and came North. There was nothing for me in that part of the country so I thought it was a good idea to join the RUC.

Epilogue

Concluding remarks can be brief because the oral testimony should stand by itself and be free from secondary interpretation and analysis. Nor does the sample permit wider generalizations being drawn. But some points are worth highlighting. There are obvious contradictions in the accounts, over such things as the trustworthiness of Catholic policemen, whether or not there was a loss of morale and indiscipline in the force, the relaxation of entry standards to join the RIC during the civil war, and on the opinion of the Black and Tans and reprisals. This merely confirms the multiplicity of standpoints that existed in the RIC and that policemen's experiences within it varied with a whole range of circumstances. Nonetheless, the oral history is consistent on many points with what is known about the period from other sources.

For example, on the whole the Black and Tans were viewed as separate from the RIC, and there was much hostility between them. As indices of this poor relationship, some members of the RIC protested to the police authorities about the policy of moving them from safe and secure Barracks in order to accommodate the soldiers and ex-servicemen, and complained about the lower standards of entry that applied to those recruited from the British Army. If not making the job of the police harder, the conduct of the Black and Tans did not help. Mr Crossett described them as pulling the RIC into bad repute, leaving ordinary policemen to stand the brunt after the Black and Tans had gone. The oral evidence also confirms that there was suspicion among some policemen about the loyalty of a minority of Catholic policemen, and the stable recruiting ground of the force remained until the end firmly located in the land and the sons of policemen. All the respondents here report the absence of other forms of employment in rural Ireland, which is why the countryside was such a good recruiting ground for America, the army and the police. Childhood memories recall poverty, lack of money and restricted opportunities for work. But the friendliness of neighbours in rural communities is also remembered. The communal solidarity, cooperation and mutual support seems to have been extended to police

128

families as well, which further disputes the idea that members of the force were not integrated into the community before the upsurge in political violence after 1916.

Other points from the oral evidence which are consistent with what is already known concern the relaxation of standards of entry after 1919, the fact that the force remained largely depoliticized and denominationally impartial, at least with respect to relations within the force, and that many policemen were unprepared and unfit for the paramilitary role which the civil war forced upon them. They were unskilled in weaponry, lacked the psychological preparedness for a military conflict, and disliked the new role. However, the young policemen whose reminiscences are reported here, evinced a more mercenary attitude toward the job, were prepared for the violence they had to confront, and claimed that it lead to no demoralization; on this last point the oral history contradicts the popular portrayal of the force. With respect to the violence, most respondents report that they 'got used to it', and came 'to live with it', even though all thought the violence not as severe as that faced today by the RUC. This tendency to claim that they adjusted to the violence might be considered an example of elderly respondents idealizing the past, but the discourse by which this adjustment is expressed replicates that of policemen and women today,[1] suggesting that there are universal processes by which members of the police normalize the danger of the job.

One other point is worth emphasizing. Even some of the younger policemen whose recollections are recorded here disliked the paramilitary role that they were required to play in the civil war. Mr McIvor, who was perhaps most heavily involved in the conflict as a member of the Reserves, stated his belief that it should be the army and not the police which provides the first line of defence in such situations, and other respondents reported their dislike of the use of guns. Thus, some expressed the belief that policemen should not be armed when pursuing ordinary crime; the colonial police model was not one which these policemen absorbed, even if it is one they practiced.

There are other features of the oral evidence which are opposed to the popular perception of the force. The political violence and conflict did not everywhere dominate police activities to the exclusion of routine policing. While some respondents reported that policing duties essentially involved the RIC versus the IRA, others continued to perform a conventional crime-fighting role, even in areas of high conflict, as Mr Crossett reports in County Tipperary. In this respect, policing at the time of the civil war and partition is similar to the RUC in contemporary Northern Ireland, where a benign role survives in many areas.[2] Nor did the political violence everywhere prevent the pursuit of an ordinary life; the danger was put at the back of their minds – there but never really contemplated. This offers another parallel with policing in Northern Ireland. The explanation for this difference in the ways in which 'the troubles' were experienced can be found in the fact that political violence in the civil war was geographically structured, such that large parts of Ireland, including the South, were relatively peaceful and encouraged a benign mode of policing. The same is true of Northern Ireland today. Thus, members of the RIC made common sense evaluations of the saftey of the places where they worked, and tended to evaluate their own as not one of the worst. There were 'good counties', which were 'quiet counties', and 'bad counties', which were 'hot spots', but even in the latter, other areas were common sensically thought of as being more dangerous. In the midst of the violence in counties Tipperary and Clare, two of the most difficult areas for policemen, the respondents concerned continued to lead as normal a life as possible, and claimed that the danger was worse somewhere else.

The oral evidence also provides a fascinating glimpse of ordinary aspects of police life at the beginning of the twentieth century. A dominant preoccupation in police research today is identifying the main lines of police occupational culture, or what Reiner calls the canteen culture of the station.[3] The concept describes the collection of values, beliefs, and practices which go to make up the occupational world of policemen. The main parameters of police occupational culture have been outlined in several studies, which point to the existence of fairly universal values and practices.[4] In this respect members of the RIC at the start of the century seem very like the policemen (and women) who are active at its close.

For example, some of the former members of the RIC emphasized their sense of camaraderie, which revealed itself in pranks, feelings of communal solidarity and the teasing of new recruits. Like policemen and women today, members of the RIC expressed a resistance to officers and formal patterns of authority within the force, and were anti-management, features which are common to workers at the bottom of large bureaucracies. Along with this, some respondents reported that they engaged in what Cain calls 'easing techniques'.[5] These are practices by which the strains and pressures of the job are reduced while at work, such as relaxing, taking time off to chat, taking one's time, and sleeping or drinking on duty.

Finally, it is worth noting that the operation of police discretion in the RIC was structured by similar processes to those today, where emphasis is placed upon the deference and demeanour of members of the public.[6] This is what policemen and women in the RUC call 'the attitude test', which is applied to people as a determinant of the course of action which the police should take. Mr Britton described the same process when he said that his action was influenced by the attitude which members of the public displayed towards him. But there are other parallels. Discretion was also influenced by the wish to avoid the unwelcome paperwork which is involved in an arrest and an unwillingness to tie up the court's time, although one respondent reported how he was under pressure from officers to obtain a quota of prosecutions; something he found difficult in a rural community in which ordinary crime was low.

Notes

Notes for Chapter 1, pp. 1–13.

1. See K. Boyle, 'Police in Ireland Before the Union: I–III', *Irish Jurist*, vol. 7, 1972, pp. 115–37, vol. 8, 1973, pp. 90–116, 323–48; S. Breathnach, *The Irish Police*, Dublin, Anvil, 1974, pp. 8–64.
2. For a selection see: T. Bowden, *The Breakdown of Public Security*, London, Sage, 1977; K. Boyle, 'Police in Ireland Before the Union: I–III', op. cit.; C. Brady, *Guardians of the Peace*, Dublin, Gill and Macmillan, 1974; S. Breathnach, *The Irish Police*, op. cit.; J.D. Brewer, 'Max Weber and the Royal Irish Constabulary: A Note on Class and Status', *British Journal of Sociology*, vol. 40, 1989, pp. 82–96; M. Farrell, *Arming the Protestants*, London, Pluto, 1983; D. Fitzpatrick, *Politics and Irish Life 1913–1921*, Dublin, Gill and Macmillan, 1977; E. Holt, *Protest and Arms*, London, Putnam, 1960; S. Palmer, *Police and Protest in England and Ireland*, Cambridge, Cambridge University Press, 1988; C. Townshend, *The British Campaign in Ireland*, Oxford, Oxford University Press, 1975; C. Townshend, *Political Violence in Ireland*, Oxford, The Clarendon Press, 1983.
3. R. Curtis, *The History of the Royal Irish Constabulary*, London, Moffet, 1869.
4. Anonymous, *Tales of the RIC*, Edinburgh, Blackwood, 1921; G. Garrow Green, *In the RIC*, London, Blackwood, 1905.
5. J. Gaughan (ed.), *Memoirs of Constable Jeremiah Mee, RIC*, Dublin, Annual Books, 1975.
6. P. Shea, *Voices and the Sound of Drums*, Belfast, Blackstaff, 1981.
7. K. Griffith and T. O'Grady, *Curious Journey: An Oral History of Ireland's Unfinished Revolution*, London, Hutchinson, 1982.
8. C. Ryder, *The RUC: A Force Under Fire*, London, Methuen, 1989, p. 14.
9. G. Palmer, *Police and Protest*, op. cit., p. 227.
10. Ibid., p. 249.
11. Ibid., p. 257.
12. See G. Fulham, 'James Shaw Kennedy and the Reformation of the Irish Constabulary, 1836–38', *Eire-Ireland*, vol. 16, 1981, pp. 93–106.
13. C. Steedman, *Policing the Victorian Community*, London, Routledge and Kegan Paul, 1984, p. 48.
14. R. Curtis, *The History of the RIC*, op. cit., p. 45.
15. Ibid., pp. 110, 117.
16. S. Breathnach, *The Irish Police*, op. cit., p. 45; C. Townshend, *Political Violence in Ireland*, op. cit., pp. 72–4.
17. S. Palmer, *Police and Protest*, op. cit., p. 29.
18. R. Sinclair, 'Retirement', *Constabulary Gazette*, September 1987, pp. 17–19.
19. J. Clarke, 'Chevrons of Three Bars', *Constabulary Gazette*, December 1986, pp. 7–11.
20. R. Curtis, *The History of the RIC*, op. cit., pp. 88–9.
21. S. Palmer, *Police and Protest*, op. cit., p. 362.

22. D. Fitzpatrick, *Politics and Irish Life*, op. cit., p. 24.
23. S. Palmer, *Police and Protest*, op. cit., p. 538.
24. G. Garrow Green, *In the RIC*, op. cit., p. 25.
25. Minutes of the Committee of Inquiry into the Royal Irish Constabulary and the Dublin Metropolitan Police, with Appendices, 1914. HMSO. Cd. 7637. Minute 1559.
26. Anonymous, *Tales of the RIC*, op. cit., p. 21.
27. S. Palmer, *Police and Protest*, op. cit., p. 332.
28. J. Clarke, 'Chevrons of Three Bars', op. cit., p. 9.
29. Minutes of the Committee of Inquiry into the Royal Irish Constabulary and the Dublin Metropolitan Police, with Appendices, 1914, op. cit., minute 6243.
30. Ibid., minute 1329.
31. Report of the Committee of Inquiry into the Royal Irish Constabulary and the Dublin Metropolitan Police, 1914. HMSO. Cd. 7421.
32. Minutes of the Committee of Inquiry into the Royal Irish Constabulary and the Dublin Metropolitan Police, with Appendices, 1914, op. cit., appendix VII.
33. Minutes of the Committee of Inquiry into the Royal Irish Constabulary and the Dublin Metropolitan Police, with Appendices, 1914, op. cit., minute 4246.
34. Ibid., minute 2300.
35. Ibid., minute 1790.
36. Ibid., minute 2856.
37. J.D. Brewer, 'Max Weber and the Royal Irish Constabulary', op. cit., pp. 93–5.
38. C. Brady, *Guardians of the Peace*, op. cit, p. 19–20; S. Breathnach, *The Irish Police*, op. cit., p. 86; D. Fitzpatrick, *Politics and Irish Life*, op. cit., p. 7; E. Holt, *Protest and Arms*, op. cit., p. 116.
39. C. Ryder, *The RUC*, op. cit., p. 25.
40. Anonymous, *Tales of the RIC*, op. cit., p. 176.
41. C. Brady, *Guardians of the Peace*, op. cit, p. 34.
42. T. Bowden, *The Breakdown of Public Security*, op. cit., p. 134.
43. C. Ryder, *The RUC*, op. cit., p. 47.
44. Anonymous, *Tales of the RIC*, op. cit., p. 178.
45. D. Fitzpatrick, *Politics and Irish Life*, op. cit., pp. 37–43.
46. C. Townshend, *The British Campaign*, op. cit., p. 92.
47. For an account of IRA tactics see T. Bowden, 'The Irish Underground and the War of Independence 1919–21', in G. Mosse (ed.), *Police Forces in History*, London, Sage, 1975.
48. D. Fitzpatrick, *Politics and Irish Life*, op. cit., p. 14.
49. Ibid., p. 17; also see C. Brady, *Guardians of the Peace*, op. cit, p. 1.
50. T. Bowden, 'The Irish Underground and the War of Independence 1919–21', op. cit., pp. 60–1.
51. C. Townshend, *The British Campaign*, op. cit., p. 75.
52. E. Holt, *Protest and Arms*, op. cit., p. 202.
53. Royal Irish Constabulary: Auxiliary Division, 1920. HMSO. Cmd. 1618. Appendix I.
54. C. Townshend, *The British Campaign*, op. cit., p. 112.
55. S. Breathnach, *The Irish Police*, op. cit., p. 90.
56. D. Fitzpatrick, *Politics and Irish Life*, op. cit., pp. 25–6.
57. P. Shea, *Voices*, op. cit., p. 66.
58. J. Gaughan (ed.), *Memoirs of Constable Jeremiah Mee*, op. cit.
59. D. Fitzpatrick, *Politics and Irish Life*, op. cit., p. 25.
60. K. Griffith and T. O'Grady, *Curious Journey*, op. cit., p. 136.
61. Quoted in D. Fitzpatrick, *Politics and Irish Life*, op. cit., p. 38.
62. M. Farrell, *Arming the Protestants*, op. cit., pp. 298–300.

63. Ibid., p. 35, passim.
64. Ibid., p. 304.
65. C. Brady, *Guardians of the Peace*, op. cit; J.D. Brewer *et al, Police, Public Order and the State*, London, Macmillan, 1988, pp. 85–107.
66. Royal Irish Constabulary: Terms of Disbandment, 1922. HMSO. Cmd. 1618A.
67. For example see: T. Bowden, 'The Irish Underground and the War of Independence 1919–21', op. cit.; T. Bowden, *The Breakdown of Public Security*; C. Brady, *Guardians of the Peace*, op. cit; M. Brogden, 'An Act to Colonise the Internal Lands of the Island', *International Journal of the Sociology of Law*, vol. 15, 1987, pp. 179–202; M. Brogden, 'The Emergence of the Police: The Colonial Dimension', *British Journal of Criminology*, vol. 27, 1987, pp. 4–14; C. Enloe, 'Police and Military in Ulster: Peace Keeping or Peace Subverting Forces?', *Journal of Peace Research*, vol. 15, 1978, pp. 243–58; D. Fitzpatrick, *Politics and Irish Life*, op. cit.; K. Griffith and T. O'Grady, *Curious Journey*, op. cit.
68. Emphasized by J.D. Brewer, 'Max Weber and the RIC', op. cit.; E. Holt, *Protest and Arms*, op. cit.; S. Palmer, *Police and Protest*, op. cit.
69. J. Tobias, 'Police and Public in the United Kingdom', *Journal of Contemporary History*, vol. 27, 1976, p. 387–402.
70. T. Bowden, 'The Irish Underground and the War of Independence 1919–21', op. cit., pp. 60–1.
71. J.D. Brewer *et al, Police, Public Order*, op. cit.; G. Mosse, 'Introduction', in G. Mosse (ed.), *Police Forces in History*, London, Sage, 1975.

Notes for Chapter 2, pp. 14–22.

1. S. Humphries, *The Handbook of Oral History*, London, Interaction Trust, 1984.
2. P. Thompson, *The Voice of the Past: Oral History*, 2nd ed., Oxford, Oxford University Press, 1988, chapter 2.
3. R. Burgess, 'Personal Documents, Oral Sources and Life Histories', in R. Burgess (ed.), *Field Research: A Sourcebook and Field Manual*, London, Allen and Unwin, 1982; K. Plummer, *Documents of Life*, London, Allen and Unwin, 1983.
4. M. Bulmer, 'Sociology and History: Some Recent Trends', *Sociology*, vol. 8, 1974, p. 141.
5. E. P. Thompson, 'On History, Sociology and Historical Relevance', *British Journal of Sociology*, vol. 27, 1976, pp. 387–402.
6. P. Thompson, *The Voice of the Past*, op. cit., pp. 64–5, 97.
7. A complaint made by R. Cormack, *Sociology*, vol. 18, 1984, p. 120.
8. P. Thompson, *The Voice of the Past*, op. cit., pp. 8, 21.
9. Ibid., chapter 3.
10. R. Munck and B. Rolstan, *Belfast in the Thirties*, Belfast, Blackstaff, 1987.
11. See J.D. Brewer, 'Looking Back at Fascism: A Phenomenological Analysis of BUF Membership', *Sociological Review*, vol. 32, 1984, pp. 742–60; J.D. Brewer, 'Micro-Sociology and the Duality of Structure: Former Fascists "Doing" Life History', in N. Fielding (ed.), *Actions and Structure*, London, Sage, 1988; L. Inowlocki, 'Denying the Past: Right Wing Extremist Youth in West Germany', *Life Stories*, vol. 1, 1985, pp. 6–14; P. Thompson, *The Voice of the Past*, op. cit, p. 2.
12. R. Samuel, 'Local History and Oral History', *History Workshop Journal*, vol. 1, 1976, pp. 191–208.
13. L. Macdonald, *They Called it Passchendaele*, London, Macmillan, 1978.
14. M. Arthur, *Northern Ireland Soldiers Talking*, London, Sidwick and Jackson, 1988.
15. M. Baker, *Cops*, London, Abacus, 1987.
16. Quoted in P. Thompson, *The Voice of the Past*, op. cit., p. 104.

17. See J.D. Brewer, 'Talking About Danger: The RUC and the Paramilitary Threat', *Sociology*, vol. 24, 1990.
18. P. Thompson, *The Voice of the Past*, op. cit., p. 53.
19. Ibid., chapter 5.
20. Ibid., p. 200.
21. P. Coleman, 'The Present in the Past', *Oral History*, vol. 14, 1986, pp. 50–7; J. Cornwall and G. Gearing, 'Biographical Interviewing with Elderly People', *Oral History*, vol. 17, 1989, pp. 36–43.
22. S. Humphries, *The Handbook of Oral History*, op. cit., p. 99.
23. P. Thompson, *The Voice of the Past*, op. cit., pp. 112–13.
24. Ibid., p. 117.
25. L. Inowlocki, 'Denying the Past: Right Wing Extremist Youth in West Germany', op. cit.
26. J.D. Brewer, 'Looking Back at Fascism: A Phenomenological Analysis of BUF Membership', op. cit.; J.D. Brewer, 'Micro-Sociology and the Duality of Structure: Former Fascists "Doing" Life History', op. cit.
27. A point made by R. Munck and B. Rolstan, *Belfast in the Thirties*, op. cit., p. 13.
28. E. P. Thompson, 'On History, Sociology and Historical Relevance', op. cit., pp. 389, 403.
29. Ibid.
30. K. Plummer, *Documents of Life*, op. cit., pp. 14–16.
31. Ibid., p. 15.

Notes for the Epilogue, pp. 128–131.

1. See J.D. Brewer, 'Talking About Danger: The RUC and the Paramilitary Threat', *Sociology*, vol. 24, 1990.
2. See J.D. Brewer, *Inside the RUC: Routine Policing in a Divided Society*, Oxford, The Clarendon Press, 1990.
3. R. Reiner, *The Politics of the Police*, Brighton, Wheatsheaf, 1985.
4. See N. Fielding, *Joining Forces*, London, Routledge and Kegan Paul, 1988; S. Holdaway, *Inside the British Police*, Oxford, Blackwell, 1983; P. Manning, *Police Work*, Cambridge, Mass, MIT Press, 1977; R. Reiner, *The Politics of the Police*, op cit.
5. M. Cain, *Society and the Policeman's Role*, London, Routledge and Kegan Paul, 1973.
6. R. Ericson, *Reproducing Order*, Toronto, University of Toronto Press, 1982, p. 17.

Selected Bibliography on the RIC

Anonymous. *Tales of the RIC*. Edinburgh: Blackwood, 1921.

Bowden, T. 'The Irish underground and the war of independence 1919–21', in G. Mosse (ed.), *Police Forces in History*. London: Sage, 1975.

Bowden, T. *The Breakdown of Public Security*. London: Sage, 1977.

Boyle, K. 'Police in Ireland before the Union: I', *Irish Jurist*, vol. 7, 1972, pp. 115–37.

Boyle, K. 'Police in Ireland before the Union: II and III', *Irish Jurist*, vol. 8, 1973, pp. 90–116, 323-48.

Brady, C. *Guardians of the Peace*. Dublin: Gill and Macmillan, 1974.

Breathnach, S. *The Irish Police*. Dublin: Anvil, 1974.

Brewer, J. D. 'Max Weber and the Royal Irish Constabulary: a note on class and status', *British Journal of Sociology*, vol.40, 1989, pp. 82–96.

Brewer, J. D. *et al Police, Public Order and the State*. London: Macmillan, 1988.

Brogden, M. 'An act to colonise the internal lands of the island', *International Journal of the Sociology of Law*, vol. 15, 1987, pp. 179–208.

Brogden, M. 'The emergence of the police: the colonial dimension', *British Journal of Criminology*, vol. 27, 1987, pp. 4–14.

Clarke, J. 'Chevrons of Three Bars', *Constabulary Gazette*, December, 1986, pp. 7–11.

Curtis, R. *The History of the Royal Irish Constabulary*. London: Moffet, 1869.

Enloe, C. 'Police and military in Ulster: peacekeeping or peace subverting forces?', *Journal of Peace Research*, vol. 15, 1978, pp. 243–58.

Farrell, M. *Arming the Protestants*. London: Pluto, 1983.

Fitzpatrick, D. *Politics and Irish Life 1913–1921*. Dublin: Gill and Macmillan, 1977.

Fulham, G. 'James Shaw-Kennedy and the reformation of the Irish Constabulary, 1836–38', *Eire-Ireland*, vol. 16, 1981, pp. 93–106.

Garrow-Green, G. *In the RIC*. London: Blackwood, 1905.

Gaughan, J. (ed.) *Memoirs of Constable Jeremiah Mee, RIC*. Dublin: Annual Books, 1975.

Griffith, K. and T. O'Grady. *Curious Journey: An Oral History of Ireland's Unfinished Revolution*. London: Hutchinson, 1982.

HMSO. Report of the Committee of Inquiry into the Royal Irish Constabulary and the Dublin Metropolitan Police, 1914. Cd. 7421.

HMSO. Minutes of the Committee of Inquiry into the Royal Irish Constabulary and the Dublin Metropolitan Police, with Appendices, 1914. Cd. 7637.

HMSO. Royal Irish Constabulary: Auxiliary Division, 1920. Cmd. 1618.

HMSO. Royal Irish Constabulary: Terms of Disbandment, 1922. Cmd. 1618A.

Holt, E. *Protest in Arms*. London: Putnam, 1960.

Palmer, S. *Police and Protest in England and Ireland*. Cambridge: Cambridge University Press, 1988.

Ryder, C. *The RUC: A Force Under Fire*. London: Methuen, 1989.

Shea, P. *Voices and the Sound of Drums*. Belfast: Blackstaff, 1981.

Sinclair, R. 'Retirement', *Constabulary Gazette*, September, 1987, pp. 17–19.

Tobias, J. 'Police and the public in the United Kingdom', *Journal of Contemporary History*, vol. 7, 1972, pp. 201–20.

Townshend, C. *The British Campaign in Ireland*. Oxford: Oxford University Press, 1975.

Townshend, C. *Political Violence in Ireland*. Oxford: Clarendon Press, 1983.

Index